The Long Freedom Road

Janet Harris

The Long

Freedom Road

The Civil Rights Story

Foreword by Whitney M. Young, Jr.

Illustrated with photographs

McGRAW-HILL BOOK COMPANY
New York · Toronto · London · Sydney

To Josie, Martin, Michael, and Clint
with special love and gratitude to Samuel Harris

Contents

	Foreword	vii
1	"The Dignity of Man"	1
2	"Be Proud of Your Race"	16
3	A Far-reaching Decision	21
4	The Montgomery Bus Boycott	31
5	The South Goes to School	46
6	Students Lead the Way— *the Sit-ins and Freedom Rides*	68
7	"I Have a Dream"	85
8	The Long Walk to the Polls— *the Mississippi Project*	102
9	The Crisis Moves North	117
10	To Fulfill the Promise of America	137
	Bibliography	147
	Index	148

Foreword

The story of the civil rights revolution is the story of many places, North and South, and of many people who were heroes. Some were leaders like Martin Luther King, and some were simply concerned citizens—such as Rosa Parks who sparked the Montgomery bus boycott, when, for reasons she cannot explain herself, she decided one day that she would not move to the back of a bus. All of these persons fought for one thing—the same rights for Negroes as for all other Americans. They fought for integration.

The fight for civil rights is called a revolution, and yet, it should be realized that integration itself is not a revolutionary thing. In reality, it is concerned with the simple fundamentals of everyday life: the right to a job, the right to a house, the right to vote, the right to an ordinary hot dog in a five-and-ten-cent store, the right to go into any movie house, the right to relieve hunger or fatigue, and to enjoy recreation facilities without fear or humiliation. These are simple fundamental rights, rights that all Americans other than Negroes take for granted. There is nothing revolutionary or complicated about such rights as these, and history has shown that persons who are segregated, either by custom or law, never acquire these rights on an equal basis.

It should also be realized that integration offers a great opportunity, not just for Negroes, but for white people. Only hopelessly insecure people want to surround themselves with sameness. Mature and creative people need and want diversity. Instead of conforming to the idea of exclusiveness, integration offers the opportunity to create the kind of society wherein people everywhere will want to apologize for sameness and boast that their churches, their businesses, their schools and their neighborhoods are like little United Nations. Not until that day will the battle for civil rights be won.

This book is a fine addition to the literature of the civil rights movement, a clear and concise account of the Negro's struggle for first-class citizenship. I recommend it highly to every young person who seeks to understand the critical issues of his own times.

Whitney M. Young, Jr.

The Long Freedom Road

"The cries of pain and the hymns and protests of an oppressed people have summoned into convocation all the majesty of this great government— the government of the greatest nation on earth."
Lyndon Baines Johnson

1   *"The Dignity of Man"*

There was no mistaking the solemn mood in the great hall where the House of Representatives meets in the nation's capital, on the chilly night of March 15, 1965. The hall, crowded with members of both houses of Congress, senators and representatives from every state in the Union, grew hushed as President Lyndon Baines Johnson began his address.

"I speak tonight," he said in his soft, Southern tones, "for the dignity of man and the destiny of democracy.

"At times, history and fate meet at a single time in a single place to shape a turning point in man's unending search for freedom.

"So it was at Lexington and Concord. So it was a

1

century ago, at Appomattox. So it was last week, in Selma, Alabama."

Selma! The name of the small Southern city was familiar to everyone in Congress. For the past three months thousands of Negro and sympathetic white people had been gathering together to pray, to march, to remind the nation that in some parts of the country only four out of every hundred qualified Negroes were able to vote.

In the Selma protest, two people had lost their lives. And two weeks later, a third would follow. On this very day of the President's address, a memorial service was being held for one of the demonstrators, the Reverend James Reeb, a young Unitarian minister.

With this fresh in their minds, many congressmen wanted to pass a voting law "with teeth in it." They listened attentively to the President.

"In our time we have come to live with moments of great crisis. Our lives have been marked with debate about great issues. But rarely in any time does an issue lay bare the secret heart of America.

"The issue of equal rights for American Negroes is such an issue. There is no Negro problem. There is no Southern problem. There is only an American problem.

"The cause of the Negro must be our cause, too.

"And we shall overcome."

"We shall overcome!" These last words, the refrain

2

of the great Negro freedom hymn, the President spoke slowly and with great emphasis.

The President's speech climaxed a decade of struggle. Although our Declaration of Independence proclaimed the founding fathers' belief "that all men are created equal," for more than three centuries American Negroes had been a people set apart, caught in a tangled web of prejudice and ignorance. They had been denied the right to vote and the right to receive equal education. They had been denied the right to full protection by the police and in the courts, often because they, like other poor citizens, could not afford good legal help. They had even been denied the right to travel freely and live and work where they pleased.

And then, in 1954, a historic Supreme Court decision sparked a mounting social revolution. All over the South and in most of the cities of the North, young Negroes began to take their grievances to the American people. Marching, picketing, praying, "sitting in" on buses, in schools, in churches, at lunch counters, and on the streets, they dramatized their plight.

Slowly, America took notice.

And now, tonight, the President had taken their rallying cry to Congress, the lawmaking body of "the greatest nation on earth," and through television, into the homes of millions of Americans.

Not for a century—not since January, 1865,

when Congress had abolished slavery in America forever by voting "aye" to the Thirteenth Amendment, which the states ratified on December 18, 1865 —had the nation been so aware of the question hidden in "the secret heart of America." Then, as now, the question was whether our democracy, founded on the principle that "all men are created equal," was to fulfill its promise.

Then, in January, 1865, the country was in the midst of a bloody Civil War, a war to save the Union and to free the Negroes from slavery. But Americans had been divided over the question of slavery since 1619, when a small ship flying a Dutch flag dropped anchor at Jamestown, Virginia, to unload the first cargo of captured Africans.

When they were brought to its shores in the seventeenth century, America was an uncultivated wilderness. To clear the forests, to plow and reap, to build villages, men and women were needed. The handful of colonists who settled America brought indentured servants from Europe. But often indentured servants ran away and disappeared into the white population. The settlers tried to hire Indians, but the red men had no use for wages and refused to work all day in the fields under the hot Southern sun.

Slavery was best suited to plantations, where unskilled labor was needed, and naturally it flourished in the South. Soon differences in attitudes widened between Northern industrial cities, where slaves were not useful, and the South, where they became necessary. At the same time, much wealth was accumulated by Northern slave traders and shippers.

Slavery was a thorn in the sides of many Americans. America was founded by people who were themselves in search of the freedom that they could not find in the Old World. Freedom was important to the early colonists who hewed out the first frontier, the east coast of America. The Revolutionary War was fought with England over the issue of freedom. Many an American agreed with President John Quincy Adams that slavery was a "great and foul stain upon the North American Union."

The Constitution contained a clause that would have permitted Congress to forbid further importation of slaves after 1808. And in the early days of the nation, it seemed slavery would eventually disappear.

Until the middle of the eighteenth century, tobacco was the principal Southern crop. Vast acreages were given over to its cultivation. Thousands of slaves were imported to tend the fields, dry the tobacco leaves, and pack them for shipping. But the fertile land yielded more than could be sold. So much tobacco was grown and shipped to Europe that the market became glutted, and prices fell. It was no longer profitable to raise tobacco. The fields lay fallow. The slaves were idle. Cotton was a less important crop because of the tedious work required to separate the soft fibers from the seeds which filled each fruit.

But then, in 1793, Eli Whitney invented the cotton gin. Cotton could now be cleaned quickly and cheaply. The South was able to compete with India and Egypt in selling it in world markets. Soon, three-fourths of the world's cotton was grown in the American South. More and more slaves were needed to grow, pick, gin, and bale cotton. The hope for an end to slavery dwindled, as "King Cotton" tightened the chains around black men, women, and children.

Working all day in the blistering fields, sleeping on corn-shuck mattresses in log shanties, living on corn pone and molasses, most slaves endured miserable lives. No wonder history records over 250 slave revolts prior to the Civil War.

The leaders of these revolts were a brave and often violent lot, and most of them came to violent ends. Denmark Vesey, a slave who had bought his freedom, promised his followers—six thousand desperate black people—that he would lead them "out of bondage and into the promised land." The revolt, in 1822, was betrayed, and Vesey was put to death. So was Nat Turner, who led a revolt nine years later.

The slave revolts added fuel to the fire of the nation's controversy over slavery. Widely circulated petitions against slavery began to appear in Congress. In January, 1836, Thomas Glascock of Georgia, a member of the House of Representatives, stated that "any attempt to agitate the question of slavery in this House is calculated to disturb the compromises of the

6

Constitution, to endanger the Union, and if persisted in, to destroy, by a servile war, the peace and prosperity of the country." In an attempt to end the controversy, Congress passed the first "gag rule"—the Pinckney Resolution—opposed by many, including John Quincy Adams. It said, "All petitions . . . relating in any way . . . to the subject of slavery shall, without being printed or referred, [be] laid on the table, and . . . no further action shall be had thereon."

Nevertheless, the petitions continued. They were chiefly the work of "abolitionists"—the small but growing band of people who believed that slavery must be abolished.

The abolitionist struggle began in the eighteenth century when such men as New Jersey Quaker John Woolman, Benjamin Franklin, and Dr. Benjamin Rush of Philadelphia, Pennsylvania, openly encouraged Negroes to seek the end of slavery. This struggle raged with increasing vigor for many years. From the ranks of the abolitionists—fiery idealists, gentle, gray-garbed Quakers, brilliant scholars, and courageous ex-slaves—came many a famous figure.

There was John Brown, demon-driven—as concerned with the Negro cause as he would have been "if his own soul had been pierced with the irons of slavery." Before his execution in Harpers Ferry, Virginia, where he had attempted to arm his followers by seizing the arsenal, John Brown said, "I have no better use for my life than to lay it down in the cause of the slave."

And there was Frederick Douglass, the former slave, whose brilliant writing and lectures took the grim story of slavery to people in Europe as well as in America.

The New England author and editor, William Lloyd Garrison, who kept his vow to be "as harsh as truth and as uncompromising as justice" in his mission, was another.

And there was Harriet Beecher Stowe. Her famous book, *Uncle Tom's Cabin* prompted Abraham Lincoln to call her "the little lady who started this great big war."

The abolitionist movement did more than challenge slavery. Freedom of speech and of the press became an issue, too, when Elijah Lovejoy founded his abolitionist newspaper in St. Louis, Missouri, in 1833. Lovejoy soon found himself in difficulties with his backers, who told him that free speech and a free press did not give him the right to "freely discuss the matter of slavery." Threatened, even hounded by mobs, he moved his press to Alton, Illinois, where again mobs attacked him. He was killed defending his rights to "determine whether the liberty of speech and of the press is to be enjoyed in Illinois."

The crusade for women's rights—a long struggle that lasted until 1920, when the Nineteenth Amendment gave women the vote—sprang from the abolitionist movement. Lucy Stone, Susan B. Anthony, Lucretia Mott, and Negro ex-slaves Harriet Tubman and Sojourner Truth tucked up their long skirts and climbed onto platforms to shout above the crowds' catcalls their belief in women's rights to go to school, to own property, and to vote.

The vexing question of slavery was hotly debated throughout the first half of the nineteenth century. The three "do-nothing" Presidents who preceded Abraham Lincoln failed to stem the deepening split in national unity that developed over this problem.

Lincoln's original position on slavery was that it was to be kept out of the new territories but left intact in the South. Yet he grew to believe strongly that the cause of the Negro was firmly tied to the very principles of our democracy. He wrote to his friend Joshua Speed: "As a nation we began by declaring that 'all men are created equal.' We now practically read it, 'all men are created equal, except Negroes.'"

The first step in freeing the slaves came early in the Civil War, when the Emancipation Proclamation was issued on January 1, 1863. It freed slaves living in Confederate-occupied territory. The Thirteenth Amendment, ratified in December, 1865, guaranteed that slavery never again would exist in the United States.

But the end of the Civil War presented new difficulties. An assassin's bullet cut down Lincoln, and Andrew Johnson, the frowning, blunt-spoken Tennes-

9

sean who succeeded him, was unpopular both in the North and the South. He was unable to bind up the serious rifts in the country.

The massive job of rebuilding the South and patching together a country torn by hate and war was difficult enough. At the heart of the matter were the four million newly freed Negroes who were now homeless, landless, chiefly unskilled and—through no fault of their own—unprepared to take their place in society.

An ex-slave described the situation:

> *"When freedom came, my mama said Old Master called all of 'em to his house, and he said, 'You all free, we ain't got nothing to do with you no more. Go on your way.' They go away and they kept coming back. They didn't have no place to go, and nothing to eat. From what she said, they had a terrible time. Some took sick and had no 'tention and died. Seemed like it was four or five years before they got to places they could live. They all got scattered. . . . Old Master every time they go back say, 'You all go on away. You been set free. You have to look out for yourselves now.'"*

Faced with increasing chaos, the South enacted the "Black Code," which, on the surface, seemed to give some rights to Negroes, but in fact virtually reenslaved them by severely regulating their personal conduct.

An "apprenticeship" system, actually another name for slavery, was established in some areas. Negroes were arrested for "loitering" and for "uppity behavior." Soon there were riots in Memphis, Tennessee, and in New Orleans, Louisiana.

The federal government passed the First Congressional Reconstruction Act, designed to protect Negroes politically and economically, in 1867. Conventions to frame new state constitutions—with some educated Negroes participating—began to meet in Southern states in January, 1868.

After the Civil War, the whites in the South had greater representation in Congress, since under law, the number of congressmen a state may have is based on its population. The Southern states now could count all the Negroes as part of the population, instead of three-fifths, as before. At the same time, the states could withhold from them the power to vote.

Like 1776—and in our day, 1954—1868 was a revolutionary year. Certain legal reforms were carried out. New public hospitals and schools were built in the South. And most important, the Fourteenth Amendment to the Constitution was passed.

The first section of the Fourteenth Amendment was designed to prevent the states from denying former slaves their rights as Americans. It stated: "All persons born or naturalized in the United States and subject to the jurisdiction thereof, are citizens of the United States and of the State wherein they reside.

11

No State shall make or enforce any law which shall abridge the privileges or immunities of citizens of the United States; nor shall any State deprive any person of life, liberty, or property, without due process of law; nor deny to any person within its jurisdiction the equal protection of the laws."

After defining citizenship, the second section set forth a penalty, loss of representation, for any state which prevented citizens from voting. The third section defined the powers of the President to pardon former Confederate leaders, and the last forbade the payment of the Confederate debt.

Two years later, in 1870, the Fifteenth Amendment declared that the right to vote could not be denied because of "race, color, or previous condition of servitude [slavery]."

For a time, the South was divided into five military districts, with a Union general heading each. With slavery ended, the large plantations divided, and the nation in the midst of an industrial revolution which demanded skilled labor and capital for building factories, the South was unable to go forward. Business floundered. Jobs and money were scarce.

A new group of "white supremacists"—people who believed that the troubles of the South could be blamed on the Negroes—rose to power when federal troops were removed from the South in 1877. White-sheeted men, members of the newly formed Ku Klux Klan, rode the country in the dark of night, striking terror into the hearts of Negroes. This and other groups, such as the Knights of the White Camellia and the Boys of '76, used violence to force Negroes back into their servile place.

Viewing Reconstruction—the period after the Civil War—today is like looking through a kaleidoscope. If you shift your eye a bit, the whole picture changes. Yet one fact is clear. The Negro won the battle of the Civil War, but lost the peace that followed it.

The emergencies of war, the collapse of the old plantation system of the South, and the North's rapid industrial expansion left little time to prepare former slaves to move into the mainstream of American life, though some of them were skilled artisans. Their former champions, the abolitionists, were of little help. Even so vocal an abolitionist as William Lloyd Garrison found the problem "solved" when slaves were emancipated, and went on to say that the freed men were not ready for "political rights and realities."

One by one, their political rights were removed. The Southern states often used roundabout methods of preventing Negroes from voting. When the Mississippi constitution was revised in 1890, it stated, "The policy of crushing out the manhood of the Negro citizens is to be carried on to success." And this policy spread throughout the South.

By the turn of the century, things were worse than they had been since the days of slavery. "Jim Crow" —the idea that Negroes must be separated from white people—became the law of the land, through legislation in the South and custom in the North. Jim Crow laws—first applied only to railroad travel in Southern states—mushroomed throughout the South. Soon there were Jim Crow laws concerning trolleys, theaters, housing, and schools.

Early in the twentieth century, Negroes began the "great migration" from the Old Confederacy to the cities of the North. Some hoped to escape Jim Crow and find better jobs. But if Negroes thought of the North as the promised land, they were soon to be disappointed. Although the "white" and "colored" signs that were tacked up in every public place in the South were invisible in the North, Jim Crow was just as much at home in New York as he was in Mississippi.

As Negroes, in ever-larger numbers, began to compete with white immigrants for industrial jobs, labor unions closed their ranks to colored workers. Having little or no protection, Negro workers could only accept lower wages, in order to live. Equally important, most of the Negroes who migrated were poorly educated, and few had the skills that were needed for well-paying jobs.

Like all other immigrant groups, Negroes who had migrated to Northern cities settled in the traditional "port of entry"—the oldest, least desirable section of the city. Not only was housing cheapest there, it was the only place where Negroes could live, for prejudice as well as poverty kept them out of the "better" neighborhoods. These older areas soon became ghettos, as white people quickly moved out.

Gradually, the North began to adopt the same Jim Crow customs that were legal throughout the South. After a quarter of a century of relatively free admission, Negroes were no longer welcomed at restaurants, theaters, hotels, and stores outside of their ghettos.

In the words of President Johnson, "the dignity of man and the destiny of democracy" were being forgotten by Americans.

2   *"Be Proud of Your Race"*

For most Negroes during the twentieth century, both in the North and in the South, the hard realities of life crowded out any theory of salvation. They were on the lowest rung of the economic ladder. All about them was prejudice. And the worst of it was that they could not look forward to a better life for their children. Jim Crow had become a firmly fixed way of life. America had erected walls between the two races —walls that most Negroes found it impossible to scale.

"Back to Africa" movements of one type or another had cropped up from time to time since 1787, when the free Negroes of Newport, Rhode Island, formed the Free African Society to promote the idea that Negroes should return to the land from which they had been brought. Shortly after the War of 1812, a Negro sea captain, Paul Cuffee, took thirty-eight Negroes aboard his brig, the *Traveller,* and set sail for Sierra Leone, in Africa.

A few years after Cuffee's expedition, the American Colonization Society was formed. Led by prominent slaveholders such as John C. Calhoun and Henry Clay, the society persuaded Congress to purchase territory in Africa. In 1820, the first group of black colonists set sail for the new country—which they named Liberia, after the word "liberty." But at the very outset the society was opposed by free Negroes and white abolitionists, and only about fifteen thousand Negroes left American shores to settle in the new "homeland."

The migration movements never caught hold, for most Negroes were not willing to abandon their hopes for equality in America, the land "so dearly bought by the blood, groans, and tears of our fathers."

But by the early 1920s, it seemed to many Negroes that there was no place for them in America, finding discrimination and segregation both in the North and in the South as they did. Many of them listened to Marcus Garvey when he urged them to leave a "white land" where "poverty is no virtue; it is a crime," and build their own civilization in Africa. "Black Nationalism," dormant for many years, gained support as Garvey told Negroes: "If you cannot live alongside the white man in peace, if you cannot get the same chance and opportunity alongside the white man, even though you are his fellow citizen . . . then find a country of your own and rise to the highest position. Africa shall be for the black peoples of the world!"

Marcus Garvey was, as he liked to boast, a "full-blooded black man" from Jamaica, British West Indies. He established his society, the Universal Negro Improvement Association, in New York City's Negro section, Harlem. Negroes crowded into Liberty Hall, where Garvey stood resplendent in a uniform of purple and gold with a helmet of feathers as "tall as Guinea grass." Surrounded by the Garvey honor guards, the Black Cross nurses, all in white, and the African Legion and the Black Eagle Flying Corps, he shouted: "Arise, you mighty race! You can accomplish what you will!"

Garvey's ambitious plan of action—the establishment of the Black Star Line, which he founded to transport Negroes to Africa—went awry. His organization mismanaged the 10 million dollars it had raised. Convicted of mail fraud, in 1923, Garvey was eventually deported to England, where he died some years later, alone and unknown. But his appeal to Negroes—"Be proud of your race!"—brought a stirring message to his people, and the cry echoed over the years in later Black Nationalist movements, such as the Nation of Islam.

The Nation of Islam—or the "Black Muslims," as its members were called—insisted that "black men and white men cannot live together in peace." All white men are "devils," its members argued. Those who believe in white supremacy are "wolves," while those who pretend to believe in equality are sly "foxes."

To achieve total separation of the races, the Black Muslims demanded that America set aside a portion of land on which Negroes could establish a separate nation. This land was owed to them, they claimed, as "back wages" for the unpaid labor of slaves and the underpaid labor of working Negroes.

Then, in 1941, America went to war again. At first, most Negro soldiers were kept carefully segregated and given menial jobs such as mess attendant. "You ain't even a second-class citizen any more," said a character in John Killen's novel about World War II, *And Then We Heard the Thunder.* "You're a second-class soldier." But in combat, segregation broke down. Later, in 1948, President Truman desegregated the armed forces by Executive order. Negroes who had been decorated for valor on the battlefield were not as likely to bow to white authority as their fathers had been. They fought alongside white men, against fascism—and racism—and they became impatient of racism in their own country. And then, too, often away from the isolation of Northern ghettos and Southern cotton patches for the first time in their lives, they began to observe new modes of living.

They began to think about the kind of life they could have if discrimination were ended.

At home, too, Negroes began to speak up. Negroes found many jobs in defense industries closed to them. A. Philip Randolph, the president of the Brotherhood of Sleeping Car Porters, spoke of assembling fifty to one hundred thousand Negroes to march on Washington to demand employment in defense industries. President Roosevelt then issued his famous Executive Order 8802, establishing a Fair Employment Practices Committee as a means of preventing anti-Negro hiring methods. The Executive order lacked any real enforcement provisions, but it was an indication that the federal government, for the first time since Reconstruction, was willing to accede to Negroes' demands.

After the war, television gained popularity. American Negroes saw the way white Americans lived. They also saw black men, in country after country in Africa, winning independence from their white colonial masters.

Cracks began to appear in the walls of segregation. But before the heart of America would soften toward the Negro, the great democratic processes of our government would have to take up the cause of equal rights for all American citizens.

It took a host of different kinds of people—ranging from a farsighted Supreme Court justice to a plucky little Kansas girl—to set the changes in motion.

3 *A Far-reaching Decision*

Eight-year-old Linda Brown liked school, even though she had to walk twenty-one blocks to get there. The long walk was bad enough, particularly on cold, rainy days. But the worst of it was that she had to walk right past another school that was only six blocks from her house.

Linda's father, Oliver Brown, wanted to transfer Linda to the closer school. But the Browns were Negroes, and so Linda, like all the other Negro children in Topeka, Kansas, in the 1950s, attended a segregated school. Linda's school was only for Negro children; the other school was only for white children.

Kansas was one of the four states that had "local option" laws. Here, as in New Mexico, Arizona, and Wyoming, each community decided whether Negro and white children could attend school together. In the seventeen Southern states, and indeed, in the nation's capital as well, the law required segregation.

But even if Linda had lived in one of the sixteen states in the North and Midwest that had laws prohibiting school segregation, or in one of the eleven remaining states, where there were no laws at all concerning school segregation, it is very likely that she would have attended an all-Negro school. Schools draw children from local neighborhoods, and in 1954, few neighborhoods in any part of the country were integrated. And so school segregation, far from being only a Southern practice, covered a large part of the country.

The more Oliver Brown mulled it over, the angrier he got. Linda had to walk across a dangerous railroad crossing twice a day. Also, her school was definitely inferior to the nearer white school. The principal did the best he could, but he could not hire the best teachers or order good athletic equipment, art supplies, or even textbooks. There simply wasn't enough money allotted by the school board. Linda wasn't getting the education her father thought she deserved.

Mr. Brown protested, but nothing happened. He discussed it with other Negro parents, and they agreed something had to be done. And so, in 1951, Oliver Brown, joined by twelve other parents of Negro children, brought suit against the Board of Education of Topeka in the United States District Court. The case was formally called *Oliver Brown et al. v. Board of Education of Topeka, Kansas.*

Mr. Brown lost his case. Troubled, he weighed his choices. There were two roads open to him. He could drop the matter and allow Linda—and thousands of other Negro children—to go on enduring the humiliation of attending inferior, segregated schools. Or he could exercise his right as a citizen of the United States and plead his case before the highest court of the land, the United States Supreme Court.

The Supreme Court had the power to reverse the District Court's decision. The judges in the lower courts, to whom Mr. Brown had already taken his case, determined that the present laws were being upheld. But the Supreme Court could decide *whether the law itself was valid or was unconstitutional.*

Oliver Brown was convinced that the entire principle of segregation was unfair. But more important, he was willing to stand by his convictions and test the law.

The Supreme Court makes thousands of decisions each year. Sometimes it takes several years before a case can be heard. By the time Mr. Brown's case "came to docket," that is, was ready to be heard, Dorothy E. Davis, of Prince Edward County, Virginia, and Harry Belton and Barbara Belton, of Dela-

23

ware, had taken similar complaints through the gamut of lower courts and finally brought them to the Supreme Court.

Oliver Brown's persistence attracted considerable attention, both in the Negro community and in legal circles. The National Association for the Advancement of Colored People (NAACP) provided him and the other Topeka parents with expert legal assistance.

Nine black-robed justices took their seats in the Supreme Court in December, 1952, to consider Oliver Brown's appeal. They had a delicate and complex problem before them. Far more than Linda Brown's schooling was at issue. Forty percent of the public school children in America attended segregated schools. Was this what the Constitution meant when it guaranteed every citizen equal protection of the laws in its Fourteenth Amendment?

And beneath this question was the unspoken one. If Negroes could not enjoy full rights, was America truly the land of freedom and equality?

Long before the middle of the twentieth century, another Supreme Court presumably had settled the question of whether separation of the races was constitutional, in a case brought by Homer Plessy, a handsome, light-skinned man who described himself as "one-eighth Negro and seven-eighths white."

By the rules of Louisiana law, Homer Plessy was considered a Negro. Louisiana had enacted a Jim

24

Crow transportation law in 1890. And so when, in 1895, Homer refused to ride in the "colored" coach of a railroad car, he was arrested.

Homer protested. "Am I not a citizen?" he asked. His rights, he insisted, were protected by the Thirteenth and Fourteenth Amendments. He was certain he had the privilege of sitting where he pleased in any public place in the country.

Homer Plessy's case came to the Supreme Court during the time that Jim Crow virtually ruled the country. Senator J. K. Vardaman had stood to announce on the floor of the United States Senate, "The Lord Almighty intended the Negro to be a menial." Bands of white vigilantes rode through the countryside. A rash of quasi-scientific books "proving" that the Negro was inferior in intelligence and morality were beginning to appear on library shelves.

By the late 1880s the notion of Negro inferiority was firmly established. The South returned to "home rule," that is, to self-rule. Southern legislatures passed a series of Jim Crow laws, and signs proclaiming "white" and "colored" became widespread.

The Supreme Court was in no mood to upset the applecart. Justice Henry Brown read the majority decision in Homer Plessy's case. He said: "The underlying fallacy" of Plessy's argument "was its assumption that the enforced separation of the two races stamps the colored race with a badge of inferiority. If this be so, it is not by reason of anything found in the act [the Louisiana law Plessy was challenging], but solely because the colored race chooses to put that construction upon it."

The Court chose to try the case on the basis of the Fourteenth Amendment. Declaring that the object of this amendment was to secure "the absolute equality of the two races before the law," the Court decided that "a law which requires the separation of the two races in a public conveyance is [not] unreasonable." Using this gauge, the Court decided that so long as the coach in which Homer Plessy rode was "equal" to the railroad car which was reserved only for white people, he had been granted his legal rights.

Homer Plessy lost his case, and America took a giant step backward. But in the gloom of that decision, there was one bright ray.

Dignified, gray-haired Justice John Marshall Harlan was appalled by the decision. He said: "Our Constitution is color-blind, and neither knows nor tolerates classes among citizens. . . . The destinies of the two races in this country are linked together, and the interests of both require that the common government of all shall not permit the seeds of race hatred to be planted under the sanction of the law. What can more certainly arouse race hate . . . than state enactments on the ground that colored citizens are so inferior and degraded that they cannot be allowed to sit in public coaches [with] white citizens? That is

. . . the real meaning of such legislation that was enacted in Louisiana."

Justice Harlan proved a wise prophet. For over a century the courts used the decision in Homer Plessy's case, *Plessy v. Ferguson,* as a yardstick, while the "seeds of race hate" sprouted like weeds. The practice of "separate but equal" grew to include schools, hospitals, restaurants, and all public and many private facilities in the South. For many years the decision remained the foundation of a house still divided.

Finally, in 1938, the first breakthrough came. The University of Missouri refused to admit Lloyd Gaines, a Negro law student, to its all-white ranks. The state made what it considered a handsome offer. If Mr. Gaines would attend a college in another state—Kansas, Nebraska, Iowa, or Illinois—Missouri would pay his tuition. He refused.

Eventually the case reached the Supreme Court. Chief Justice Charles Evans Hughes, who had run against Wilson for the Presidency in 1916, wrote that the state of Missouri could not deny to Negroes the education offered to whites. It was, he insisted, the duty of Missouri, "when it provides legal training, to supply it to the residents of the state upon the basis of the equality of right."

Nine years later, a young Texas Negro named Sweatt applied to the University of Texas Law School. He was rejected because of his race. Young

Mr. Sweatt was allowed, instead, to enroll in a hastily constructed annex to the University.

Mr. Sweatt was exasperated. The "new University" had no real library and only a part-time faculty. It wasn't even an accredited school. What would he do with the diploma he earned from such a "University?" No client would ever hire him! He, too, took his case to court.

When his case, *Sweatt v. Painter,* was heard by the Supreme Court, the justices unanimously agreed with him. The University could pull no such tricks, they decided. Mr. Sweatt was to be admitted to the University proper immediately.

But in none of these cases did the Supreme Court come squarely to grips with the constitutionality of the "separate but equal" doctrine. The cases of Gaines and Sweatt raised only one question: were the states offering Negro students the same kind of education as they offered to white students, and so living up to the letter of the law, as established in Homer Plessy's case?

Oliver Brown's lawyers presented the crucial problem to the Court. Was not the entire practice of "separate but equal" in itself unconstitutional, they asked. And by 1954, many people throughout the country were asking the same question.

When the Supreme Court is in session, every Monday is a red-letter day in its lofty main room. For

Monday is the day on which the justices announce their decisions on cases. But no one who was in the courtroom on Monday, May 17, 1954, could remember a day in which the very air had been so alive with suspense and excitement.

Supreme Court decisions are usually announced to the press via a pneumatic tube which runs from the courtroom to the press chamber. But this time, no light flashed to indicate a printed decision. Reporters were invited to "come to the courtroom."

Facing the reporters and spectators in the crowded room, Chief Justice Earl Warren reviewed the three questions the court had had to decide in making its decision:

1. Is the doctrine of "separate but equal" constitutional?
2. Even though the facilities in segregated schools are equal, does not the mere fact that the schools are segregated deprive Negro children of an equal education?
3. If children are separated because of race, does that separation cause a Negro child to feel inferior to a white child?

First Chief Justice Warren noted that when the Fourteenth Amendment granted Negroes citizenship in 1865, public education had not been a central concern of government. But, in Justice Warren's words,

"Today education is probably the most important function of state and local government."

The Chief Justice continued to the second question, which he put in these words: "Does segregation of children in public schools solely on the basis of race . . . deprive the children of the minority group of equal educational opportunities?" The question hung in the air. "We believe it does."

In answering the third question, Justice Warren spoke of the generations of Negro children who had been educated in segregated schools. "To separate them from others of similar age and qualifications because of their race generates a feeling of inferiority . . . that may affect their hearts and minds in a way unlikely ever to be undone.

"We conclude that in the field of public education . . . segregation is a denial of the equal protection of the laws."

Within hours, all America knew the results of the case. *The New York Times* called the unanimous decision "a monumental and constructive stride in constitutional law and fundamental justice."

Oliver Brown won his case.

"I woke up this mornin' with my mind set on freedom. Hallelu, hallelu, hallelujah."

4 *The Montgomery Bus Boycott*

There is no plaque in Montgomery, Alabama, as there is at Bunker Hill, to mark it as the birthplace of a revolution. Yet as surely as the shots fired on Bunker Hill were heard round the world, the steady footsteps of Montgomery's Negroes walking to their jobs during the whole year of 1956 echoed through America.

In the Negro revolution, as in the American Revolution, the idea of freedom was dramatically translated into action. Montgomery was not the first site of such action. Insurrections, mass movements, and riots of one sort or another had erupted periodically in many places, in many guises, since 1658, when slaves in Connecticut rebelled, killed their masters, and fled to live among the Indians.

31

But the quiet revolution that began in Montgomery was different from the hundreds of earlier flareups. Montgomery became the testing ground for a new means of revolt—"nonviolent protest."

How did it all come about? What exactly is nonviolence? Who were the people in the story? What sort of a place is Montgomery? What were the reasons for the revolt?

Montgomery, the capital of Alabama, is a traditional Southern city. It was once the capital of the Confederacy. Jefferson Davis, the President of the Confederacy, stood on the portico of the Capitol there to receive the oath of office. There the Confederate flag was first unfurled.

Montgomery is also a modern city, with large office buildings and with a section of the business district devoted to state administration. It is an important center for cotton, livestock, and lumber, but there is little heavy industry. Because there are few jobs available, most Negroes find menial positions as domestic workers, porters, or unskilled laborers. There is a small class of Negro professionals, but most Negroes in Montgomery are poor.

Though the United States Supreme Court had decided in 1954 that segregation—in schools, at least —was unconstitutional, in only a few places, such as Washington, D.C., had any changes occurred. Like every other Southern city, Montgomery was as strictly segregated in 1955 as it had been since the end of Reconstruction.

There were separate schools for white and for Negro children. Separate restaurants, barber shops, and theaters served the white community and the Negro community. There were special playgrounds, parks, and swimming pools for whites. Negroes were not admitted to "white" wards in hospitals. Even the toilets and water fountains in public places were marked "white" and "colored," and no thirsty Negro youngster dared to drink from the "white" spigot!

Nowhere were the lines of segregation harder to cross than on the local buses, where the front of each vehicle was strictly reserved for whites, the rear for Negroes.

One of the daily riders of these segregated buses was a Negro woman named Rosa Parks. On December 1, 1955, tired from her day's work as a seamstress in a downtown department store, she boarded a bus to travel home.

She was lucky because there was an empty seat. With a sigh of relief, she sat down and eased her aching feet out of her snug shoes.

After a few stops, the bus became crowded. Mrs. Parks looked up to find a white man standing over her. He demanded that she give up her seat.

Mrs. Parks hesitated. It was against the law for a Negro to refuse such an order. Yet almost as though it were not her own voice, she heard herself answer, quietly but firmly, "No, I'm sorry."

The driver stopped the bus and called a policeman. Within a few minutes, Mrs. Parks was arrested, booked, and put into jail.

In a matter of hours, many of Montgomery's Negroes heard the news. Mrs. Parks was popular and well known. She had been secretary of the local NAACP. She had helped organize church suppers and bazaars, and she was a familiar figure at prayer meetings.

As they spread word of Rosa Parks's arrest, people remembered what had happened the year before. Claudette Colvin, a pretty Negro high school sophomore, had also refused to surrender her seat on a bus. She, too, was whisked to jail. The Negro community attempted to change the system. They appointed a citizen's committee to talk to the manager of the bus company and to the Montgomery City Commission, which ran the local government.

The bus company officials and the police commissioner, representing the city commission, said they were sorry about what had happened and promised changes. Claudette was tried, found guilty, and given a suspended sentence. The changes promised by the city commission never came about.

Now, Mrs. Parks's friends decided, enough was enough! The Supreme Court had supported Linda Brown's right to attend school with her white playmates. The pattern of "separate but equal" had been challenged in the Supreme Court, and the Supreme Court had ruled segregation unconstitutional. It was time for the segregation on Montgomery's buses to end too!

Later that evening, E. D. Nixon, a burly former Pullman porter who had been president of the Alabama NAACP, signed bond for Mrs. Parks. As soon as he saw her safely home, he started telephoning the other leaders of the Negro community.

Early the next morning, he called the new minister of the Dexter Avenue Baptist Church. Without so much as a "Hello," Nixon plunged into the story of Mrs. Parks's arrest. "We have taken this type of thing too long already," he said, his voice shaking with emotion. "The time has come to boycott the buses. Only through a boycott can we make the white folks understand that we will not accept this kind of treatment any longer."

It was a fateful telephone call. The man to whom E. D. Nixon spoke that morning was the Reverend Martin Luther King.

Martin Luther King was then twenty-seven years old. He was born in Atlanta, Georgia, the son of a minister and grandson of a sharecropper. Once, when he was a small boy, his father took him to a downtown shoe store. They sat down in the first empty seats, in the front of the store.

A young white clerk went over to them and said

politely, "I'll be happy to wait on you if you'll just move to the rear of the store."

"We're comfortable *here*," his father replied.

"Sorry," said the clerk, "but you'll have to move."

"We'll either buy shoes sitting here, or we won't buy shoes at all," Reverend King replied, and taking Martin by the hand, he walked out of the store. "I don't care how long I have to live with this system," he said angrily to his son. "I will never accept it."

Martin Luther King knew he could never accept it, either. He worked hard in school. He went to Crozer Theological Seminary in Chester, Pennsylvania, and then to Boston University. While he was studying in Boston and taking additional courses in philosophy at Harvard, he met a beautiful girl, Coretta Scott. She was a music student at New England Conservatory. They were married in 1953.

Coretta King's home was in Marion, Alabama. She, too, grew up with prejudice. So when young Dr. King was offered the pastorate of the Dexter Avenue Church, deep in the South, they both knew what their problems would be. Coretta would have little opportunity for a singing career in Montgomery. Their children would have to attend segregated schools. But the young couple decided to return to the South. As educated Negroes, they felt a moral obligation to help their people acquire real freedom and equality.

The Dexter Avenue Baptist Church to which Dr.

King came is a handsome red brick building standing on one corner of a square near the center of downtown Montgomery. There were influential and respected citizens in the congregation. Like many Southern churches, this church was more than a place in which to worship God, it was a community center as well.

The planning meeting for the bus boycott was called for 7:30 P.M. on Friday, December 2, the day after Mrs. Parks was arrested. When Dr. King entered the large meeting room, he found it already filled. In the room were physicians, schoolteachers, lawyers, businessmen, postal workers, union leaders, and clergymen—people from every segment of Negro life—all of them willing and anxious to lend their support to the boycott.

The committee worked feverishly that night and the following day. Telephones hummed as news of the boycott spread through the community. A committee of women mimeographed leaflets, to be distributed by Monday, when the boycott was to begin:

DON'T RIDE THE BUS TO WORK, TO TOWN, TO SCHOOL, OR ANY PLACE MONDAY, DECEMBER 5.

ANOTHER NEGRO WOMAN HAS BEEN ARRESTED AND PUT IN JAIL BECAUSE SHE REFUSED TO GIVE UP HER BUS SEAT.

DON'T RIDE THE BUSES. IF YOU WORK, TAKE A CAB, OR SHARE A RIDE, OR WALK.

COME TO A MASS MEETING, MONDAY AT 7:00 P.M. AT THE HOLT STREET BAPTIST CHURCH FOR FURTHER INSTRUCTION.

Dr. King was up and dressed by 5:30 Monday morning. At 6 his wife called to him, "Martin, come quickly." The first bus had gone by—and it had been empty!

Together they watched the second and the third bus. Not a single Negro passenger!

On December 5, 90 percent of the Negroes who usually rode the buses stayed off them.

Bus after bus, empty except for a handful of self-conscious white passengers, rolled down streets crowded with domestic workers and laborers patiently walking miles to work.

Children ran and leaped after the buses, shouting "No riders today!"

Policemen on motorcycles trailed the buses. In the white community, the false rumor spread that "goons," strong-armed Negroes, were to prevent Negroes from boarding the buses.

The bus boycott was a tremendous success that Monday. Now Dr. King and his associates had to make a decision. Should they continue the boycott? Perhaps it would be better to call it off rather than run the risk of a fizzle. But when they reached the Monday night mass meeting, arranged by Ralph Abernathy, minister of the Holt Street Church, their fears were quelled.

Traffic was jammed for five blocks around the building. In the dark night, police cars circled the church. People, ten deep, stood quietly on the streets outside the packed church. Loudspeakers were hooked up to the outside of the building.

As he walked into the church, Dr. King hesitated. He had not had the time to prepare a speech, and he had much to say. Dr. King wanted his people to know that this boycott was not like the other boycotts that had been used in the South. White segregationist groups had often boycotted Negroes who had asked for fair treatment by "blacklisting" them. Once branded a "troublemaker," a Negro was not likely to be able to find work. White businessmen who were in sympathy with Negroes had been boycotted, too, and as a result of campaigns by segregationists, some of them had been unable to keep their businesses going.

But this boycott was different. "Our concern," Dr. King said later, "was not to put the bus company *out* of business, but to put *justice in business*. We are saying to the white community: 'We can no longer lend our cooperation to an evil system.'"

To change the "evil system," Dr. King proposed a program of nonviolent protest or resistance. It was a philosophy he had come to believe in while he was still a theological student. It was derived from the Sermon on the Mount: Love thine enemy. It had roots in Thoreau's theory of civil disobedience: Take dramatic action to protest unfair laws. And finally, it had been spelled out in the theory of passive resistance, as conceived by Mahatma Ghandi in India's successful struggle for independence from Britain.

Dr. King knew he was asking his people to embark on a difficult path. Would his people walk quietly and not give in to anger even if they were jeered at and beaten? Could they win the understanding of the segregationists? Could the Negroes accept suffering without returning hurt for hurt? Could they end hatred—simply by refusing to re-create it? If they gave in to violence, Montgomery would be the home of one more futile, bloody episode.

With these thoughts in mind, Dr. King climbed the platform to the pulpit. And there he found he needed no prepared speech. The words came from his heart:

"There comes a time," he said, "that people get tired."

"Yes, yes," the people murmured.

"We are tired of being segregated and humiliated."

"Amen."

"Tired of being kicked about."

"Yes, yes."

"We have no alternative but to protest. We are protesting for the birth of justice in the community. In our protest there will be no cross burnings. No white person will be taken from his home by a hooded Negro mob and brutally murdered. There will be no threats and intimidation.

"Love must be our ideal. Love your enemies, bless them, and pray for them. Let no man pull you so low as to make you hate him.

"If you will protest courageously, and yet with dignity and Christian love, when the history books are written in future generations the historians will say, 'There lived a great people—a black people—who gave new meaning and dignity to civilization.'"

The Negroes of Montgomery voted for brotherly love and for protest. They voted, that night, to ask for courteous treatment by the bus operators; to ask to be seated on a first-come, first-served basis, with Negroes seated from the back of the bus and whites seated from the front; and to ask for Negro bus drivers on mainly Negro lines. They voted to stay off the buses until their demands were met.

The boycott continued, for the modest requests made to the bus company were not granted. The walkers trudged on. Private car pools were organized. A druggist volunteered to dispatch cars from a downtown parking lot. A fleet of fifteen new station wagons was added, each car registered as the property of a different church, with the church name written on it. Every morning as these wagons carried their loads of passengers to work, startled passersby heard the sound of hymn singing drifting from the open windows!

The costs of operating the boycott were enormous. Help poured in—first dimes and nickels from the Negroes of Montgomery, then contributions from all over the world. Donations came from Tokyo, from Singapore. The largest donations were made by church groups, both Negro and white.

The owners of the bus company grew panicky as they saw only empty buses and empty coin boxes. In desperation, the city officials acted. On February 22, 1956, Dr. King and nearly one hundred others were arrested on a charge of "conspiracy to conduct an illegal boycott." Friends posted bail, and the boycott leaders returned to their work while they awaited trial.

Another meeting was held, this time in the First Baptist Church. Dr. Abernathy, Dr. King's close friend, officiated. Two thousand people attended.

"Do you want to keep on walking?" Dr. Abernathy asked the boycotters.

"Yes, yes!" they shouted.

In March, Dr. King was convicted and fined $1,000. Eventually the fine was paid, and the other cases were dropped, but the arrests increased the determination of the boycotters.

Violence fed the boycott, too. In contrast to the

quiet behavior of the strikers, the segregationists responded with acts of terror. Four Negro churches were bombed on January 10, along with the houses of two ministers—one white, one Negro. On January 30, Dr. King's house was bombed. Although the family was home, miraculously no one was hurt.

By March, Dr. King's house had been bombed three times. "Kill me, but know that if you do, you have fifty thousand more to kill," Dr. King warned from his pulpit.

Spring came, bringing with it drenching, warm rain. The boycotters continued to walk. A reporter questioned one of the walkers, a tiny, bent old woman. "Aren't you tired?" he asked.

"My feets is tired," she said softly. "But my soul is rested."

Some whites preferred to place the blame on Communists and outside agitators. Many a domestic, quietly attending to her tasks in the home of her white employer, was questioned about the movement. One Negro girl described the situation: "Our white families [employers] say to us, it's such a terrible thing that a man like that Reverend King comes here and gets the colored people all stirred up, and we say, 'No, ma'am, the reverend, he didn't stir us up, we've been stirred up a mighty long time.' But our white folks, they just don't seem to hear us."

But the voices of Montgomery's Negroes were heard—in the courts, as well as on the streets. An appeal by Aurelia Browder, who, like Mrs. Parks, had been arrested and convicted for refusing to comply with "Jim Crow" bus regulations, was filed in the United States District Court. When the Court ruled against bus segregation, Montgomery's officials took the case to the United States Supreme Court.

Mrs. Browder's lawyers questioned whether or not a community could establish and enforce Jim Crow laws, since the Supreme Court had ruled in favor of Oliver Brown in the school segregation case. And the Supreme Court, on November 13, 1956, agreed that segregation was just as illegal on buses as it had been in schools. The state laws which required segregation on Montgomery's buses were declared invalid. The Montgomery boycotters had won their case!

On December 20, more than a year after Rosa Parks's arrest, the decision reached Montgomery, and the buses were desegregated. Dr. King, Dr. Abernathy, E. D. Nixon, and the Reverend Glenn Smiley, a white Southern ally, rode the first integrated bus.

The bus driver greeted the group with a warm smile as they took their seats in the front of the bus. "We are glad to have you with us this morning," he said.

The success of the bus boycott was an important victory for civil rights, though the fight was just beginning. The victory went far beyond the original battle for a bus seat. The boycott was a way for Negroes to express the feelings that they could not put into words.

"We are tired of being segregated and humiliated," Dr. King had thundered from his pulpit. "We will walk the streets until the walls of segregation are finally battered by the forces of justice." And Negroes listened, and were aroused. They followed the leader who taught them to protest against poverty and injustice through the persuasive power of brotherly love. When Martin Luther King was awarded the Nobel Prize for Peace eight years later, it was as "the first person in the Western World to have shown that a struggle can be waged without violence."

The boycott focused the attention of white Americans on their colored fellow citizens. Public opinion, spurred on by acts of civil disobedience such as the Montgomery boycott, was shifting. Though most white citizens were preoccupied with their own affairs, changes were taking place, not only on the streets of the South but in the Supreme Court and in the halls of Congress where the law of the land was decided.

5   *The South Goes to School*

For Jo Ann Allen and eleven other Negro youngsters who had just been admitted to the previously all-white high school in Clinton, Tennessee, September, 1956, was a banner month.

The eight hundred white students cheerfully accepted their Negro classmates. In fact, members of Jo Ann's ninth-grade class described her as "pretty and smart, with a wonderful personality," and promptly elected her homeroom vice-president. Neither Jo Ann nor most of the teachers and students knew that on the streets outside the school trouble was brewing.

During the preceding year, several hundred districts throughout the country had simply closed their shabby all-Negro schools and sent children of both races to the previously all-white schools.

Border states, such as Kansas and Arizona, with small Negro populations, were able to desegregate easily. President Eisenhower turned the District of Columbia's schools into a showcase for integration. Baltimore, Maryland, with one of the largest segregated school systems in the country, promptly integrated its schools.

In the Deep South—in states such as Mississippi, Alabama, Georgia, and Louisiana—matters were different. Here, segregation had been held over since slavery days, and the white people did not like the idea of what they termed "mixing the races."

Even so, at first, most of the South seemed to be willing to accept the new laws. Most people agreed with Virginia's Governor Thomas B. Stanley, when he said: "We will work toward a plan which will be acceptable to our citizens. Everyone is just trying to find a solution for what they regard a major problem."

In this spirit, the town fathers of Clinton had arranged the integration of the high school. Now some of them were worried. They knew that a stranger from New Jersey, twenty-six-year-old John Kasper, had quietly arrived in town the week before.

Kasper had slipped into a telephone booth in a Main Street drugstore and had begun to dial numbers at random from the phone book. "The niggers got to be pulled out of the high school," he whispered ominously. "We're calling a meeting—you better come!"

Most of the people whom he reached told him to hang up and stop bothering decent folks. But Kasper was not easily put off. He buttonholed people in the stores. He called a meeting in front of the town's war memorial. "The Communists want to see the colored man going to school with white boys and girls. Are you a Christian or a Communist?" he harangued. The crowds began to stir uneasily.

The board of aldermen met and told Kasper to leave town. He refused, and was arrested. After a night in jail, he returned to the streets. Arrested a second time, he was released on bond, but he continued to agitate until, at last, he succeeded.

A crowd of white men and women began to gather at the high school each morning. They shouted insults at the students. Negro children were chased. Their white classmates watched, dumbfounded.

Saturday night the crowd, now an enraged mob of three thousand, gathered in the downtown section of Clinton. Many local Negroes, fearing the worst, piled their families hastily into cars and left town. Clinton's seven-man police force was powerless against the crowd. But on the outskirts of town, Leo Grant, a young Florida-born lawyer and Korean War hero, swiftly moved into action.

"We just up and formed a posse," he said later. "Forty-seven of us—preachers, doctors, clerks. You never saw such a collection of weapons . . . a German burp gun . . . plenty of double-barreled shotguns, and we got from the mayor of Knoxville two machine guns and six tear-gas grenades."

The grenades did the trick. The volunteers, in a skirmish line, divided the crowd in two. Leo hurled a gas grenade; the mob moved back. Rallying, with shouts to kill, the crowd moved forward again. Then 110 state highway patrolmen poured in to keep order. The following day, the National Guard arrived, and an uneasy truce came to Clinton.

The responsible citizens of Clinton continued to fight mob violence and saved both the town and the school system. A Knoxville judge and jury found Kasper and six others guilty of violating the Federal District Court's desegregation order. In all, it was a victory for law and order—and fair-minded people—in the South.

Unfortunately, Clinton's hard-won peace was only temporary. Two years later, the integrated high school was destroyed by dynamite. And this kind of defiance of the law was repeated over and over in the South.

Most white Southerners regretted the Supreme Court decision. They had no love for integration. Although, like people throughout the country, they believed deeply in the American creed—liberty, justice, and equality—many of them did not understand that Negroes in America could not really participate in our democracy. Busy with their own affairs, they did little for the civil rights cause. For those who did care, this inactivity was another block to overcome.

Many white Southerners simply went along with the bland assumption that "our Negroes are happy. They don't want things changed." The walls of segregation were so firmly fixed that Negroes and whites were scarcely able to communicate with each other. They did not understand each other's problems. Many whites found it hard to believe that Negroes were not satisfied with the old Southern system.

Even so, most white people in the South would have bowed to the inevitable changes brought about by the Supreme Court decision in the Brown case. They would have heeded the reasonable voices of those like the town fathers of Hoxie, Arkansas who believed that people of goodwill could work together for racial harmony—if it had not been for the goading of the newly formed White Citizens Councils.

The White Citizens Councils were made up of extreme segregationists. "The Negroes have organizations," they argued, "so it's time for *us* to band together." They went to school board and civic meetings to fight integration. They took full-page ads in local papers. They saw to it that Negroes who fought for their rights were fired from their jobs and put out of their homes.

Most effective of all their methods was the pressure the councils placed on local and state governments, directly and indirectly.

Responding as politicians do to pressures, even

Governor Stanley revised his stand. "I shall use every legal means," he said, "to continue segregated schools in Virginia." Other states followed suit.

One hundred and one Southern senators—the entire Southern bloc, except for Senator Lyndon Johnson and both senators from Tennessee—signed the "Southern Manifesto" of 1956. The paper called the Supreme Court decision "clear abuse of judicial power," and pledged "massive resistance to integration."

This "massive resistance" soon became the pattern of the South. Some communities closed their schools denying to *all* children the right to an education. Other communities gave in to terror and lawlessness.

Both the White Citizens Councils and the local political leaders wanted to keep the federal government from moving in. They clung to the principle of "states' rights"—pointing out that the states, rather than the national government, had the responsibility for administering the schools.

Nobody anticipated trouble in Little Rock, Arkansas. The school board had worked for three years on a gradual integration plan, which seemed to satisfy most people. It was to start with the admission of a few Negro children to Central High School on Tuesday, September 3, 1957.

Then the unexpected happened.

On Monday night, September 2, Arkansas Governor Orville Faubus made a surprise television address. He said it would not be possible to maintain order if Negro children tried to enter the high school. The battle lines began to form.

The next morning, as early as six o'clock, there were handfuls of men and women gathered in front of the school. One hundred state troops, Arkansas National Guardsmen sent by Governor Faubus, were also there. Some sat on the edge of the sidewalk, some sprawled on the hard cement, their rifles and bayonets lying beside them.

"It looks kinda quiet," one guardsman said.

"Just think, we're making history!" another said.

"Not me," his khaki-clad companion retorted. "I'd rather go fishing than make history in this hot sun."

Slowly, a crowd gathered. By eight o'clock, there were more than one hundred men and women standing across the street from the school. Most of them were in a happy mood. "We sure kept the Niggers out," one said. "They won't dare show their faces here."

A half hour later, nine Negro children, led by fifteen-year-old Elizabeth Eckford, tried to enter the school. As they rounded the corner, they saw more than four hundred white people. Guarding the entrance to the school was a taut line of guardsmen, their rifles and bayonets raised.

A shout went up from the crowd. "A nigger! Here they come!"

Elizabeth followed some white students past a

guard toward the school door. Another guard pushed her back and barred the door with his bayonet.

"I turned around," she said later. "The crowd came toward me, yelling 'Lynch her! Lynch her!'" She thought she saw a friendly look on the face of an old woman, but when she approached her, the woman spat.

A guard officer led her to a bench at the bus stop. A white woman, comforting Elizabeth, put her arm about her. The crowd catcalled. "She's just a scared little girl," the woman cried angrily to the mob. "Aren't you ashamed?"

Another Negro youngster advanced to the school grounds. He was Terrence Roberts, who had transferred from all-Negro Horace Mann High School, where he was a straight-A student.

The guards formed a human fence and did not let him pass. "Keep away from our school, you burrhead!" a spectator shouted.

Terrence turned to one of the guards. "I was told if there is any resistance and I am not permitted to go in, not to try to force my way."

"Are you scared?" a reporter asked.

"Yes, I am," he replied. Then he said, "I think the students would like me okay once they got to know me." He shrugged and walked away.

The following day, the Federal Bureau of Investigation (FBI) sent agents to Little Rock.

The Arkansas state troops stayed at Central High

for three weeks. Then Little Rock's Negroes, backed by the NAACP, won a court order forcing Governor Faubus to withdraw the state troops. When the school opened the following Monday, a mob of over a thousand greeted the nine Negro students. The segregationists climbed over police barriers and into the school. At noon, a local police lieutenant evacuated the Negro students through a side door.

That evening President Eisenhower who believed firmly in the principle of local control, invoked a law written in 1871 and sent a thousand United States Army paratroopers to Little Rock. For the first time since Reconstruction, federal troops were ordered to protect the rights of Negroes. Negroes could now count on federal intervention if states failed to protect their safety.

Elizabeth Eckford and the others went back to Central High, this time in Army jeeps! For the rest of the school year, the federal soldiers remained on duty. Inside the building, the students learned English, math, and science as usual, while the cries of the mob and the tread of paratroopers' boots outside filtered in through the open windows.

The real heroes and heroines of Little Rock were the nine Negro students and the great majority of the white students. Except for about 150 of the nearly 2,000 white students, the student body of Central High heeded the school newspaper's plea to "accept the situation without demonstration." Not one student leader, nor a single member of Central High's championship football team, the "Tigers," went along with the segregationists. White and Negro students sat next to each other in classes and walked through the halls together.

The National Broadcasting Company assigned a Norwegian correspondent, Mrs. Jorunn Ricketts, to interview some of the young people in the integrated school. Six Central students were on the program. There were three white girls, Sammy Dean Parker, Kay Bacon, and Robin Woods; one Negro girl, Minnijean Brown; one white boy, Joseph Fox; and one Negro boy, Ernest Green. Here is some of the conversation:

Mrs. Ricketts: "Do you think it is possible to start working this out on a more sensible basis than violent demonstrations?"

Sammy: "The South has always been against racial mixing, and I think they will fight this to the end. We fight for our freedom. And we don't have freedom any more."

Ernest: "Sammy, you said that you don't have freedom. I wonder what you mean by freedom. You are guaranteed your freedoms in the Bill of Rights and your Constitution. You have the freedom of speech—I noticed that has been exercised a whole lot in Little Rock. The freedom of petition, the freedom of religion, and the other freedoms are guaranteed to you. As far as freedom, I think that if anybody should kick about freedom, it should be us."

Sammy: "Do you call those troops freedom?"

Ernest: "Why did the troops come here? It is because our state government went against the federal law. Our country is set up so that no one state can overrule our nation's government. I thought that was what our country was built around. I mean that is why we fight. The fellows I know fought and died in World War II, in the Korean War. Why should my friends get out there and die for a cause called democracy when I can't exercise my rights, tell me that!"

Robin: "I agree with Ernest."

Joe: "Well, Sammy, I don't know what freedom has been taken away from you, because the federal troops haven't kept me from going to my classes. They're just there to keep order in case the hotheads get riled up. I think if parents would just stay out of it and let the children at Central High figure it out for themselves, it would be a whole lot better."

Sammy: "I think we knew before this ever started that some day we were going to have to integrate the schools. And I think the Governor was trying to protect all of us when he called out the National Guard."

Ernest: "Well, I have to disagree. . . . When Elizabeth walked two blocks with the mob behind her, did the troops break up the mob?"

Robin: "When Elizabeth had to walk down in front of the school, I was there and I saw that. I was very ashamed—I felt like crying—because she was so very brave. And we were just jeering her. I think that we shouldn't have acted that way. If everybody would just obey the golden rule—do unto others as you would have others do unto you—it might be the solution. How would you like to have to walk down the street with everybody yelling behind you like they yelled behind Elizabeth?"

As Mrs. Ricketts continued the interview, the discussion turned toward the young people's understanding each other. Mrs. Ricketts asked the white students whether they had ever made an effort to find out what Negroes are like. Kay and Sammy said they had not, until today.

Kay: "Well, you know that my parents and a lot of the other students and their parents think that the Negroes aren't equal to us. But—I don't know. It seems like they are, to me."

Sammy: "These people are—we'll have to admit that."

Ernest: "I think that if the people of Little Rock would get together and discuss their views, instead of getting out in the street and kicking people around and calling names, it would be smoothed over."

Kay: "I think that if our friends had been in this discussion today, I think that maybe some of them would change their minds. We came down here today with our minds set against integration. I know now that we're going to change our minds."

For a time, integration seemed to be a tug-of-war between Negroes, with their chant "Freedom now!" and the segregationists, wearing large campaign buttons militantly proclaiming "Never!" Then, gradually, a third force began to emerge. This was made up of "moderates," men and women who realized that integration was now the law of the land, and who made plans to save their communities *before* they became battlegrounds.

Atlanta, Georgia, was a town in which the moderates were able to make their voices heard. Atlanta's citizens began to take gradual steps toward peaceful desegregation.

First, the library's main branch admitted Negroes. Many restaurants were desegregated. Parks and recreational facilities were opened to both races. White and Negro community leaders formed councils, in which they could work out compromise solutions to their problems.

Atlanta resolved not to follow the lead of such states as Virginia, by closing its schools, or of Little Rock, by permitting mob rule to take over. A group of housewives formed an organization aptly named HOPE (Help Our Public Education), in a drive to keep schools open and functioning smoothly.

Common sense marked Atlanta's attitude. Perhaps it was best stated by Chief of Police Herbert Jenkins, who was training his men to aid, not resist, school integration. "I am prepared to yield to the judgment of the Supreme Court. Why? Because as law enforcement officers, there is no other position we can honestly take."

When school opened in Atlanta in 1961, there were no chanting mobs, no threats of lynching. The Negro youngsters who had been transferred to four previously all-white schools were welcomed by their classmates with smiles and handshakes.

If cooler heads had prevailed, more citizens would have reacted as did those in Atlanta. But still more crises were in the making. In the outbursts of terror, segregationists were to discover, to their dismay, that the federal government was ready to take even larger steps to protect citizens' rights than it had in Little Rock.

In 1962, eight years after the Supreme Court decision, there were still three states—Alabama, Mississippi, and South Carolina—in which *no* Negro and white students attended public school together. To crack the stronghold of segregation that was Mississippi would take a person of courage, ability, and unusual determination.

James Meredith was just such a young man. One of ten children born to a poor Attala County, Mississippi, farmer, he had earned credits toward a college degree while serving as a staff sergeant in the United States Air Force. He was exactly the kind of young man the University of Mississippi preferred to have as a student—except for the fact that he was a Negro.

When James Meredith was twelve, he visited the office of a white physician whom he admired. The doctor was a graduate of the University, which was familiarly called "Ole Miss"; and when James noticed a picture of the doctor, wearing an Ole Miss football uniform in his college days, the boy decided he himself would like to attend the University one day.

James Meredith was not one to accept humiliation passively. When he was a little boy, he refused the nickels and dimes that an eccentric white man used to pass out on the streets to Negro children. "I considered it degrading," he said.

When he was fifteen, he took a train trip to visit relatives. "The train wasn't segregated when we left Detroit," he said, "but when we got to Memphis, the conductor told me I had to go to another car. I cried all the way, and in a way, I've been crying ever since."

Such experiences gave James Meredith the determination to continue to apply to the University and to fight through some thirty legal actions before he was admitted. He applied to the NAACP and to the federal government for aid, and it was given to him. At last the United States government entered the case as "a friend of the court," and his application was accepted.

At this point the Governor of Mississippi, Ross Barnett, went on statewide television to make public his policy of defying segregation orders. "I hereby direct each official to uphold segregation laws enacted by the state of Mississippi, regardless of the federal courts," he said.

On the morning of September 20, 1962, when James Meredith appeared on the University campus at Oxford, Mississippi, to register, he found the doorway blocked. Standing before him was the Governor himself.

"Do you have any business before the University?" the Governor asked.

James answered steadily, "I came here to enroll in the University."

University Registrar Ellis read a proclamation adopted by the University trustees naming Governor Barnett acting registrar. Governor Barnett promptly told Meredith his application for admission was denied.

The campus was already prepared for riots. Students had been gathering all day, some standing beside a Confederate flag, and many shouting: "Two four six eight! We don't want to integrate!"

But the riots did not take place that day, nor did they take place on September 25, when James Meredith, flanked by a Justice Department attorney and the Chief United States Marshal, again was refused admission. Again and again, enrollment was denied him.

President John F. Kennedy made a series of three telephone calls to Barnett, the last at midnight of September 28. Then, he called Mississippi's National Guard into federal service and dispatched United States Army troops to Memphis to stand by for active duty if needed.

On Sunday night, September 30, Meredith was flown back to the University from Memphis in a federal plane. Deputy Attorney General Nicholas Katzenbach met him at the airport, and he was driven to the campus in a convoy of military trucks.

That night President Kennedy made a national television address directed to the students at Ole Miss. "You have new opportunity to show [your] patriotism," he said. "The most effective means of upholding the law is not the state policemen or National Guard. It is *you*."

His pleas fell on deaf ears. Even as the President was speaking, a riot was raging on the campus. The 320 federal marshals who had been sent to the University to see that the court order was obeyed were attacked by a mob of white students and townspeople. Flaming missiles, rocks, bricks, and acid were thrown at them. The marshals fought back with tear gas.

President Kennedy and his brother, United States Attorney General Robert F. Kennedy, ordered federalized National Guardsmen and United States Army units to the campus. Transport planes and helicopters brought them in.

When the sun rose on the littered campus, the rioters retreated. Two men had been killed during the night. One was a correspondent for a French news agency, the other a spectator from nearby Abbeville, Alabama.

James Meredith stayed on at the University of Mississippi. He attended all his classes in the company of federal marshals who had been assigned to protect him by President Kennedy.

For a time, the strain seemed to be too much for young Mr. Meredith, and the rumor circulated that he was failing in his studies. Hearing this, he commented, "A Negro should have the same right to fail as a white student."

James Meredith received his hard-won diploma in 1963, nine years after the Supreme Court school desegregation decision. The Supreme Court had anticipated that many problems would arise in local communities as each was faced with the prospect of integrating its schools. For that reason, the Court did not set a time limit for desegregation. It only recommended that integration proceed "at all deliberate speed."

The executive branch of the federal government did not foresee the need to use force in the school issue. President Eisenhower had described the attitude of the federal government when he said, before the Little Rock crisis, "I can't imagine any set of circumstances that would call for federal intervention." But the events that took place required the federal government to step in, not to integrate the schools, but to protect Little Rock's citizens.

Many people, both in the South and in the North, questioned this role of the federal government. Under our Constitution, all powers *not given specifically to the federal government* (nor prohibited to it) are *reserved to the states*. The schools are not mentioned in the Constitution, and therefore should it not be the states' responsibility to handle all school matters? This explains why some people asked whether the federal government was infringing on states' rights. Other people wondered whether the states were responsible enough to handle school integration *without* bringing the federal government into the picture. The latter group got its answer when Clemson College in South Carolina enrolled its first Negro student.

Harvey Gantt, a twenty-year-old Negro who planned to major in architecture, had been admitted, by a court order, to the college. For several weeks before the enrollment date of January 28, 1963, people were asking if South Carolina had learned from the tragic lesson at Ole Miss.

Behind the scenes, as early as 1961, some of South Carolina's businessmen had begun a drive to pave the way for peaceful desegregation. "The desegregation issue cannot continue to be hidden behind the door. We have a definite obligation to our Negro citizens," one of the group said. The others, including Governor Hollings, agreed.

Governor Hollings spoke to the South Carolina Assembly about desegregation. He told reporters: "Before 1962 has passed, South Carolina's legal defenses will fall like a house of cards. Prepare your readers for the inevitable. We are *not* going to secede!"

The Governor sent the head of the state's law enforcement division to Ole Miss during the riots to study law enforcement methods in riot control. He wanted to be sure that South Carolina could handle any trouble on the campus without assistance from the United States Army.

But despite careful preparations, nobody could be sure that Klansmen would not descend upon the

Clemson campus, burning fiery crosses, fighting, spreading terror and death.

The campus seemed calm enough. One student commented: "Everybody feels just the same. They're not in favor of Gantt being here, but there's nothing that can be done about it."

Another expressed a different opinion: "If Gantt comes here to study, he can study. If he comes to goof off, he'll flunk out. I think he'll be welcomed. If I pass him on campus, I'll say 'Hi' to him."

When the day finally came and Harvey Gantt drove up to the administration building, he was greeted by a crowd of 150 newspapermen and 150 students.

As he walked to the door, flashbulbs popped. Someone shouted: "Smile! You're on 'Candid Camera.'"

Gantt laughed merrily. "Is that right?" he replied.

Later that day, Harvey was welcomed by the college's president. He ate dinner in the college cafeteria, and although no one sat with him the first day, several students walked over to him and greeted him warmly.

There was quite a difference between the bloody reception James Meredith received at the University of Mississippi and the calm and pleasant one Harvey Gantt found at Clemson. Responsible business and political leaders and, most of all, an intelligent school administration and student body proved that Southern schools could be integrated with dignity.

During the next decade, through a combination of legal moves and social protest, Jim Crow began to lose ground in the classroom. And it was in the segregated South, rather than in the "integrated" North, that the greatest changes were made, for in the South, segregation had been established by *law*. So new laws, such as the Civil Rights Act of 1964, and new interpretations of existing laws could be used to end segregation. In the North, where segregation had grown up *outside the law* legal methods were not so effective.

The Civil Rights Act of 1964 brought a new weapon with which to fight Jim Crow in schools. It permitted the federal government to withhold funds from those schools that did not comply with integration guidelines established by the U.S. Office of Education. By May, 1966, nearly 1,500 school districts in the Southern and border states had pledged to meet the Office of Education's standards, while only 255 had ignored the request that the standards be met.

As late as the spring of 1966, the vast majority of Negro children in the South still attended all-Negro schools. In Alabama, for example, only three Negro children out of every thousand attended schools with white classmates. But in Texas, once totally segregated, one out of five Negro children went to an integrated school. The progress in school integration was slow, but every year more schools were being integrated.

> *"For the first time in our history, a major social movement, shaking the nation to its bones, is being led by young people."*
>
> *The New Abolitionists*—Howard Zinn

6 Students Lead the Way— the Sit-ins and Freedom Rides

On a cold January afternoon in 1960, Joseph Mac-Neill, a freshman in a Negro college in Greensboro, North Carolina, stopped in at the downtown bus terminal. "I'd like a hamburger and a cup of coffee," he said.

The waitress looked past him. "We don't serve Negroes," she called over her shoulder.

Joseph was not surprised, but he was angry. On his desk, back at the dormitory was a letter from a student organization in a South Carolina Negro college. "We want the world to know," it said, "that we no longer accept the inferior position of second class citizenship. We are willing to go to jail, to be ridiculed, spat upon and suffer physical violence to obtain first class citizenship."

Joseph felt that way, too. So did Ezell Blair, his room-mate. They were part of a new generation of Negroes who had grown up during the years following the Supreme Court decision of 1954. They knew about, and had seen, Negro children who bravely had walked past angry mobs to take their places in white schools. They had seen Negroes of all ages—working-men in coveralls, women, some carrying children in their arms, and old people—trudging miles to work rather than ride Montgomery's Jim Crow buses.

And now Joseph and Ezell thought it was their turn!

Joseph MacNeill decided to return to the lunch counter where he had been refused service. "Let's have a sit-in," he proposed to Ezell. "Let's ask to be waited on, and just sit there until they bring our food!"

The next day Joseph, Ezell, and two of their friends, all neatly dressed in freshly pressed suits, took their seats at the lunch counter.

The waitress refused to serve them, and the white customers glowered at them, but the young men continued to sit quietly at the counter. After two hours, they silently filed out of the store, joined hands to form a circle, and, standing in front of the store, recited the Lord's Prayer together.

The local radio station interrupted a program of music to broadcast news of the sit-in. Soon other stu-

69

dents, both white and Negro, flocked to the luncheonette to carry on the demonstration.

The boys did not realize that the Greensboro sit-in would spread from town to town like a chain reaction. Within three months there would be hundreds of similar demonstrations, in every Southern and border state, and some in the North as well. The boys did know, though, that before the angry murmurings they heard at the luncheonette turned into mob violence, they would need help.

A committee of students called upon Dr. George Simpkins, head of the Greensboro NAACP. Dr. Simpkins listened, a thoughtful look on his face. Then he placed a call to the New York office of CORE (Congress of Racial Equality).

Both the NAACP and CORE had organized sit-ins. The NAACP had opened lunch counters in Oklahoma City, Oklahoma, in 1958. CORE had staged sit-ins since 1940, in Northern cities and then in border cities such as Baltimore and St. Louis. Although these demonstrations had simply sprung up here and there and had not spread, Dr. Simpkins believed that CORE was ready to use its money and experience to help in what promised to be a new mass movement.

CORE sent Len Holt, a Norfolk, Virginia, lawyer, to Greensboro to train the students in nonviolent protest. Soon the youngsters were participating in the strangest classes any of them had ever seen!

A long table, representing a lunch counter, was set

Following the eruption of violence in Watts, Los Angeles, members of the California National Guard stand watch over the deserted streets.

After signing the Voting Rights Bill on August 6, 1965, President Johnson gives to Dr. Martin Luther King the pen with which he signed the historic document.

WIDE WORLD PHOTOS

In Birmingham, Alabama, Negroes registered protests in street demonstrations in 1963.

During the summer of 1966, carrying banners demanding "Black Power," this group of CORE members picketed the main post office in Philadelphia, Penn.

The lot of Southern sharecroppers was often harsh. In 1939, these men, unable to find work picking cotton, faced starvation.

Arkansas state troopers escort nine Negro students to the front door of Central High School in Little Rock.

To integrate the New York City schools, Negro pupils (such as those in the photograph) were bused from Harlem to Yorkville.

Leaders of the Washington March are shown here with President Kennedy. From left to right, Whitney M. Young, Jr., Dr. Martin Luther King, John Lewis (rear), Rabbi Joachim Prinz, Dr. Eugene Blake, A. Philip Randolph, President Kennedy, Walter Reuther, Vice President Johnson (rear), and Roy Wilkins.

up. Each student took his seat and "ordered lunch." Len Holt played the part of a white onlooker. As he walked along the counter, he pushed the students, blew smoke in their faces, rubbed ketchup and mustard into their hair, and called them names.

At first, most of the students were able to ignore him, but when Len hit them and shoved them from their chairs, some fought back. Those who raised their fists or returned insult for insult were immediately flunked out!

These "dress rehearsals" continued for several weeks. Students who possessed good self-discipline and control were deemed ready for nonviolent action. They were sent back to the streets, armed only with their own determination, their rigorous training, and mimeographed instructions to "Dress neatly," "Turn the other cheek," and *Do not fight back!*" Others continued to attend the classes, while hotheads were advised to drop out of nonviolence classes and stay away from the sit-ins!

Greensboro became the site of an important civil rights conference. Leaders of the three major civil rights organizations—the NAACP, CORE, and the Southern Christian Leadership Conference (SCLC), the organization born of the Montgomery bus boycott—met in Greensboro.

The NAACP was the pioneer organization. It had been formed in 1909 by a few veteran abolitionists and Negro intellectuals, including the Negro writer

71

and educator, Dr. W. E. B. DuBois, to protest the lynching of a Negro in Springfield, Illinois. Pledged to stand for "the rights of man, irrespective of race or color, for the highest ideals of American democracy," it soon found itself in the forefront of the battle for civil rights.

The NAACP's well-trained lawyers have traveled all over the country to defend Negroes caught in the tangle of unfair legal practices. The NAACP lobby, in Washington, works to bring about legislation to better the lot of Negroes and provides information and services to congressmen. The organization has worked steadily and effectively toward the four goals it was founded to work toward: abolition of enforced segregation, equal education for Negroes and whites, voting rights for Negroes, and the enforcement of the Fourteenth and Fifteenth Amendments.

In the early 1960s, the NAACP had nearly half a million members. There was scarcely a Southern town or city that did not have an active chapter. It was the largest of the Negro leadership groups, efficiently run and well organized.

CORE, too, was an active organization, though it was much smaller in scope and membership than the NAACP. Based mainly in the North, it had only a few staff members in the South. CORE's members were engaged in direct action, rather than courtroom battles. Since its beginning in the 1940s, CORE had successfully desegregated many housing projects and restaurants in New York and Chicago, Illinois. The organization knew more about sit-ins than any other group and had more calls for help and leadership than it could answer.

The NAACP, CORE, and the Southern Christian Leadership Conference gave advice and aid to Greensboro students. But as the newspapers and television reports flashed the news of the Greensboro sit-ins and more and more college students followed Joseph's and Ezell's lead, the young people realized that they wanted their own council, one that would permit them to be as imaginative, independent, and creative as they liked.

Easter vacation seemed to be the perfect time for the students to get together. They met in Raleigh, North Carolina—142 of them, from forty Southern campuses.

"This is the most significant gathering ever held in America since the Constitutional Convention," one young man said. Perhaps this was an exaggeration, but the students didn't think it was. They were certain they had a vital mission.

The result of the Easter conference was the formation of the Student Nonviolent Coordinating Committee (SNCC). An office was set up in a tiny, windowless cubicle in downtown Atlanta, with one part-time worker to send out bushels of mail and answer the constantly jingling telephone. A humble beginning indeed, but it would not be long before SNCC became a focal point in the whole Southern civil rights movement.

SNCC held meetings once a month, beginning in the spring of 1960. Representatives were elected, one from each Southern state, to make plans for direct action. John Lewis, a short, stocky young divinity student from a small town in Alabama, was elected chairman, and James Forman, an intense twenty-five-year-old schoolteacher, became executive secretary.

Now backed by an organization of their own, the students took matters firmly into their own hands. The Greensboro sit-ins continued; it took just six months to integrate Woolworth's lunch counter! And during that time, segregation began to lose ground all over the South.

In some towns, civic leaders saw what was taking place in Greensboro and in countless other towns. "Colored" and "white" signs were quietly removed *before* demonstrations took place. In other towns, students took part in demonstrations. The sit-ins spread to hotels, movie theaters, and parks. "Wade-ins" were organized to integrate pools and beaches. Sunday mornings saw "pray-ins" to open white churches to Negro worshippers.

The South was astounded by the efficiency of the organizers. "It just seems that these things start overnight," a store owner lamented. "You don't even know where all those kids come from."

They came from a peaceable army of several thousand volunteers, well organized and ready at a moment's notice to cut classes and to travel to any town where they might be needed.

Some people dismissed the student demonstrators with a shrug. "A bunch of crazy kids out to make trouble," one said. How surprised these critics would have been if they had been behind the scenes of a sit-in! Here, for example, is the schedule followed by a group of students whose purpose was to integrate ten downtown restaurants in Atlanta, in October, 1960:

By 8 A.M., the basement of a centrally located church was already filled with the first contingent of volunteers. About forty students sat down at a long table. Over coffee and doughnuts, they made plans for the day's activities.

Then, heads bowed, the students prayed for guidance. "Let us be nonviolent. Let us be loving. And open the hearts of the American people to our cause."

A stack of neatly typed papers was distributed. The papers contained reports of the previous day's progress. After these were reviewed, it was time to choose students to demonstrate that day. Assignments were made according to each student's class schedule, and each volunteer selected the type of action he preferred.

Transportation—private cars and station wagons —began to arrive at 9 A.M. The drivers were handed lists of locations and street directions.

Now the students went out "on duty." Headquarters kept careful track of them, via walkie-talkies and telephone calls. Meanwhile, gifts arrived at the church. A Negro storekeeper brought a carton of food; a housewife arrived with two pies, still warm from the oven. A service station operator called to ask, "Do you folks need some gas for transportation?"

The students returned to the church late in the afternoon. Eagerly they listened to each other's tales and described their own experiences. Once again prayers were said, and then, weary but cheerful, the young people returned to their dormitories and homes.

By November, 1960, some 155 communities had been host to direct-action demonstrations. It seemed as though the TV screens showed the same scenes over and over again. There were the lunch counters with a dozen or so young Negro students patiently waiting to be served. Milling around them were angry hecklers. Sometimes police whistles screamed and sirens whistled as carloads of students were taken off the picket lines and to the jails.

Television cameras brought the civil rights story to white America. Television had become a two-way communication. The Negro revolution had started partly because Negroes were able to see for themselves the kind of life open to white people in our country; now whites were able to see for themselves the grievances of Negroes.

Changes, often invisible to onlookers, were taking place. Sometimes a student silently walking with a picket sign that said "Freedom Now" or "We Shall Overcome" would be surprised to hear a white passerby whisper, "Keep it up; we're with you."

"Many a Virginian must have felt a twinge of regret," read an editorial in the Richmond, Virginia, *News-Leader*. "Here were the colored students in coats, white shirts, and one was taking notes from a biology text. And here on the sidewalk outside was a gang of white boys come to heckle—a ragtail rabble, slack-jawed, black-jacketed . . . fit to kill . . . waving the proud flag of the Confederacy. . . . It gives one pause."

The sit-ins were taken up by Northern students, too. A few weeks after the Greensboro demonstrations began early in 1960, the Youth Council of the NAACP called a "sympathy demonstration" in Englewood, New Jersey. And several days later, ten University of Wisconsin students, dressed in heavy parkas and fleece-lined boots, braved subfreezing temperatures to picket the Madison, Wisconsin, branch of Woolworth's. "We will not patronize stores whose Southern outlets discriminate," their leaflets said.

By the middle of March, there had been demonstrations in Newark, New Jersey; Washington, D.C.;

Boston, Massachusetts; Los Angeles, California; and Seattle, Washington. Students from colleges and universities in every part of the country—Princeton, Vassar, Yale, Harvard, Antioch, Queens, the University of Indiana, the University of Chicago, and the University of California at Berkeley among them— saw their share of demonstrations.

The students in the North mainly were white, rather than Negro, and sometimes they picketed in cold rain and snow, while the Southern youngsters walked in the pleasant sunshine of an early spring. But the scenes the Northern students described were often similar.

A white student from Smith College, in Northampton, Massachussetts, wrote: "We started, about 75 of us, from 24 states and Ghana, in front of the library. We went down through the wet, sloppy snow to the business section, handing out mimeographed letters of support for the sit-ins in the South. There were snowballs thrown at us, but not an awful lot. A couple of people called 'Nigger lovers,' but some people clapped when we walked by."

The student leaders hoped to reach the consciences of people all over America. Now it began to seem they had. The CORE offices in the North were soon swamped with young people, both white and Negro, eager to volunteer their services. CORE decided it was time for the movement to "take to the road."

Five years earlier, during the Montgomery bus boycott, the Supreme Court had declared segregation illegal on any public transportation vehicle. But the decision left an important question open. What happens after a Negro leaves his bus, train, or plane? Suppose he wants to use the waiting room, rest room, or restaurant in the terminal? If these facilities were owned by the carrier—the plane, bus, or railroad company—the answer was clear: federal laws prohibiting segregation on interstate carriers made Jim Crow illegal in the terminals, too. But if a private company owned a restaurant in a bus terminal, for example, did it have the right to reserve one area for whites and another for Negroes?

A young Negro law student named Bruce Boynton decided to find the answer to that question. He took a bus from Washington, D.C., to Montgomery, Alabama. It stopped in Richmond, Virginia, for a forty-minute layover. Mr. Boynton sat down on a stool in the "white" section of the lunchroom and ordered a sandwich and a cup of tea. He was arrested, tried, and convicted. Eventually, the case was appealed to the United States Supreme Court.

The Supreme Court's decision, made in 1960, said that since the terminal and its restaurant and other facilities were part of the bus company's service—even though the bus company did not own these facilities—under the federal Interstate Commerce Act, Negro passengers were entitled to the same rights in the terminals which they had on the buses.

CORE knew from experience that a law on the books was quite different from a law in practice. Negroes and whites would continue to use separate waiting rooms out of fear and force of habit unless demonstrators "opened" the facilities through direct action. And so, in the spring of 1961, CORE launched the "freedom rides."

None of the original thirteen passengers on the Washington–to–New Orleans "freedom bus" on May 4, 1961, knew what kind of incidents would occur.

The interracial group—six whites and seven Negroes, including James Farmer, director of CORE—were well aware of dangers they faced. They had spent three days in nonviolence classes before leaving, and by the time the bus left, they felt like old friends. To keep their courage up, they sang freedom songs, laughed, joked, and chatted about the civil rights movement.

The first three days were uneventful. A dispute at the Danville, Virginia, Trailways terminal over restaurant service was settled amicably. Then the drama began to build.

A Negro rider was arrested when he asked for a shoeshine in a Charlotte, North Carolina, bus terminal. And by the time one of the buses (for eventually there were three of them) arrived in Rock Hill, South Carolina, a mob was waiting.

John Lewis, the young SNCC leader, was the first to get off the bus. "I knew it was going to be bad," he said later. But resolutely squaring his shoulders, he went into the "white" waiting room. There he and two white freedom riders were savagely beaten by a gang of hoodlums.

The worst was still ahead, in Anniston and Birmingham, Alabama. Acting on a tip, State Investigator Eli Cowling had boarded one of the Greyhound buses to protect the freedom riders. Just outside Anniston, the bus was ambushed.

Cowling barred the bus door as an angry crowd tried to attack the passengers. But the enraged mob, shouting "Get them!" was not to be stopped. A fire bomb was hurled through an open window, and in moments the bus was ablaze.

Handkerchiefs covering their faces, the freedom riders ran through the smoke and flames. All were bruised and beaten, and twelve of them were hospitalized. Behind them, the abandoned bus burned to charred embers on the red dirt embankment.

In Birmingham, some 60 miles away, a similar fate awaited another busload of freedom riders. James Farmer, who had left the bus at Atlanta to attend his father's funeral, had sent a telegram to Attorney General Robert Kennedy asking for federal protection. The Justice Department immediately telegraphed Birmingham Police Chief "Bull" Connor and asked that he send his men to protect the riders when the bus arrived.

"Bull" Connor chose to disregard the request. "I

have said that these out-of-town meddlers are going to cause bloodshed if they keep meddling in the South's business," he responded.

When the bus pulled into the Birmingham terminal, the riders were greeted by some one hundred enraged people. And not a policeman was in sight!

Mayhem followed. The freedom riders headed for the "white" waiting room. They were waylaid, dragged into an alleyway, and beaten.

Bruised but determined, the freedom riders voted to continue to their destination. But no bus driver would finish the hazardous trip! The group took a plane to New Orleans.

The next week, a biracial group of students left Atlanta on another freedom bus, with Montgomery as their destination.

President Kennedy and his brother, the Attorney General, faced a difficult choice, just as President Eisenhower had during the Little Rock episode in 1957. On May 21, after weighing the alternatives open to the federal government, the Attorney General sent a force of five hundred federal marshals to Montgomery, over the protests of Alabama's Governor Patterson. "The United States Government needs assurance by action—not words—that its citizens will be safe in the State of Alabama," he wired the Governor.

The freedom bus sped toward Montgomery. Then, federal marshals mounted jeeps and transport trucks and headed for the Alabama capital. The bus got there first.

As the small group of riders disembarked at the bus terminal, an angry crowd surged forward to meet them. A race riot involving hundreds broke out. For two hours the streets of downtown Montgomery exploded. Newspaper reporters, photographers, passersby—all were caught up in the fray. Montgomery police were sent in. They fired pistols over the heads of the rioters to quiet them. It was not until the federal marshals arrived that peace was restored.

New groups of volunteers replaced the original riders. Their destination was Jackson, Mississippi. Early on the morning of May 24, a bus carrying twelve freedom riders—eleven Negroes and one white—left Montgomery. National Guardsmen lined both sides of the street near the bus terminal. A few hours later a second freedom bus left; its destination, too, was Jackson.

Later that day, as the first group of riders got off the bus in Jackson, they found policemen waiting for them. The riders began to walk toward the "white" waiting room. "Are y'all here to make trouble?" one of the officers asked.

"No. We're here to integrate the terminal," a rider answered.

"Then y'all are under arrest," the policeman said.

All summer long the freedom buses rolled South. The jails of Jackson and Parchman State Prison in

Mississippi filled to overflowing. Among those arrested was a young Negro girl. Friends who visited her found her brutally beaten. Her face was so swollen she had difficulty speaking. But she managed a small smile, and one word: "Freedom."

By the end of the summer, more than three hundred freedom riders had come to the Deep South. Three-quarters of them were from the North, and half of them were white. Eventually, more than one thousand people took this hot, dusty journey.

As a result of the freedom rides, the Attorney General's Office realized that the Supreme Court decision in the case of Bruce Boynton (*Boynton v. Virginia*) was not enough to end Jim Crow in terminals. The Attorney General asked the Interstate Commerce Commission for sweeping orders preventing segregation in bus and rail travel. Four months later, in November, 1961, the Commission issued regulations. The Justice Department carefully investigated the country's airports and found fifteen with segregated facilities. Thirteen desegregated voluntarily, and the other two desegregated after suits by the Justice Department. By 1963, Attorney General Kennedy was able to say, "Systematic segregation of Negroes in interstate transportation has disappeared."

More than new laws followed the freedom rides and the sit-ins. The young people had fired the nation with their own spirit. Now not only Negroes but young white people, too, felt that they had a stake in the new movement.

7   *"I Have a Dream"*

The "long hot summer of 1963" began with two rifle shots on a lonely stretch of highway near Gadsden, Alabama, in April, and ended in the nation's capital on August 28, with a "gentle army," black and white, a quarter of a million strong, massed along both sides of the reflecting pool at the base of the Lincoln Memorial.

In the South, there had been many demonstrations. In the North, young people had protested bias in labor unions by demonstrating at construction sites. They had blocked the movement of bulldozers and trucks by sitting down in their paths. They had picketed and boycotted schools, places of business, and housing projects.

The plight of the Negro, so dramatically demonstrated across the nation, pricked the consciences of many Americans. Although most Americans failed to do anything, some white people were strong champions of equal rights for Negroes. They were willing to stand up and be counted. They were willing to take risks for the cause they felt so deeply.

William Moore, a white mailman from Baltimore, Maryland, decided "it's time we Southerners solve our own problems and get rid of the black eye when it comes to race relations." To do this, he decided, he would go on a "one-man freedom walk" through the South, speaking directly to people and spreading his message.

Moore packed some clothing, an extra pair of shoes and some civil rights pamphlets into a small shopping cart. He set out with two letters, each pleading for action on civil rights. One was addressed to President Kennedy, the other to Mississippi's Governor Ross Barnett. On his back he wore a sandwich board that said, "Eat at Joe's both Black and White," and "Equal Rights for All (Mississippi or bust)."

As he continued on his lonely trek, many people stopped to hear his views. Some agreed with him. But many were angry, and some threw rocks at him. Near Gadsden, Alabama, on April 23, 1963, he was interviewed by a radio newsman. The reporter asked him whether he feared violence.

"I don't believe the people in the South are that way," he replied. The reporter was worried about him, and so was a state investigator who drove up to offer him a lift. But Moore declined the offer and went on his way.

Early that evening, he made some notes in his diary: "Walking again. Traffic cop waved greeting. Invited to chat with a few men who heard about my walk on T.V. They didn't think I'd finish my walk alive. . . ."

Four hours later a motorist found his body in front of a roadside park. He had been shot in the forehead and neck, at close range, with a .22 caliber rifle.

The news of Moore's death, widely broadcast on television, shocked the nation. Civil rights groups decided that others would continue the march that William Moore had started. Eight Negroes left Birmingham and drove to Attala, Alabama, where they planned to start their walk. They, too, carried signs that said "Equal Rights for All." They were arrested within a few minutes by a deputy sheriff.

At the Alabama border, another group of marchers —five whites and five Negroes who had set out from Chattanooga, Tennessee—saw a battery of state patrolmen waiting to arrest them as soon as they set foot over the state line. The marchers began to sing:

"I woke up this morning with my mind set on
  freedom.
I woke up this morning with my mind set on
  freedom.
Hallelu, hallelu, hallelujah.

"Oh, we'll walk, walk, walk, walk,
With our mind on freedom.
Oh, we'll talk, talk, talk, talk,
With our mind on freedom,
Hallelu, hallelu, hallelujah."

They were still singing when the state policemen arrested them and carried them to waiting police cars.

Still the marches continued. Another group set out for a memorial service at the roadside park where Bill Moore's body was found. One of the speakers at the service was a white man from Chattanooga. "I've come here to make amends for everything that's been going on down here for the last 200 years," he said.

During the early months of 1963, civil rights leaders had been meeting to discuss the choice of a new site for a large-scale demonstration. Now, in April, there was more reason than ever for direct action.

In January, President John F. Kennedy had said that he did not intend to press Congress for additional civil rights legislation in 1963. As the tempo of the struggle increased, and the issues became clearer, he decided to ask Congress to pass a new civil rights law.

The young people who were shaping America's destiny wanted a sweeping law—one that would end Jim Crow in public places and remove barriers to equal rights in housing, employment, and education and at the polls. To achieve this, the civil rights movement would have to rivet the eyes of the nation on the conditions under which Negroes lived. Perhaps if Americans could see these conditions for themselves, they would demand that changes be made and stronger laws be written. With this hope, civil rights leaders, headed once again by Martin Luther King, chose Birmingham, Alabama, for the next demonstration.

Birmingham, the steel-producing city of the South, was labeled "the most segregated city in America." "In Birmingham," *The New York Times* reported, "whites and blacks still walk the same streets. But the streets, the water supply and the sewer system are the only public facilities they share. . . .

"Neither whites nor blacks talk freely. A pastor carefully closes the door before he speaks. A Negro keeps an eye on the sidewalk outside his house. Telephones are tapped. . . . Mail is intercepted . . . the eavesdropper, the informer, the spy have become a fact of life. Every inch of middle ground has been [blocked] by the whip, the razor, the gun, the bomb, the torch, the knife, the mob, the police and many branches of the state's apparatus."

The target in Birmingham would be Jim Crow in all public places—schools, restaurants, department stores, parks, auditoriums. Job discrimination was to stop so that Negroes could be hired on an equal basis. And to help Birmingham settle its racial problems peacefully in the future, a biracial panel of community leaders was to be set up.

Thirty thousand Negroes and a handful of whites took part in the Birmingham marches. Most of them were young people, and many thousands were school-age children as young as six or seven years.

Some people criticized Dr. King for letting small children march. They thought that the children were in danger. Dr. King's answer was, "Children face the stinging darts of segregation as well as adults." A Negro mother said, "These younger people are not going to take what we took."

When Chief of Police "Bull" Connor put up barricades to stop the marchers from crossing a street, the children sang:

> *"Ain't gonna let Bull Connor*
> *Turn me round*
> *Turn me round*
> *Turn me round,"*

and a new song written in memory of William Moore:

> *"I'm going to walk for William Moore.*
> *Goin' to walk the streets of Gadsden*
> *I'm going to walk all over 'Bama*
> *We will never turn back*
> *We are marching on to freedom*
> *Black and white together."*

Throughout April, the streets of Birmingham were filled with demonstrators, singing freedom songs, marching, picketing, kneeling to pray. Each day thousands were dragged from the streets and to jail.

Jail was no threat. The children expected to be jailed. Handbills were distributed near the Negro schools each morning. "Fight for freedom first, then go to school." The instructions read: "Join the thousands in jail who are making their witness for freedom. It's up to you to free our teachers, our parents, yourselves and our country."

As days went by, white priests, ministers, and rabbis from all over the country came to Birmingham to lend their support. One of them, Rabbi Seymour Friedman of New York, taught the marchers a song from the book of Psalms. "Behold how good and how pleasant it is for brethren to dwell together in unity" were the words. One afternoon, Rabbi Friedman led the march. Behind him were three thousand Negroes, carrying signs that said "Freedom Now" and singing fervently—in Hebrew!

Dr. King repeatedly asked the demonstrators to remain nonviolent. Most of them followed instructions. But as the atmosphere became more bitter, nonviolence faltered.

On May 3, police watched a small park fill with demonstrators. They brought out the police dogs and the fire hoses that they used to turn back the marchers. As the policemen adjusted their hoses, a Negro boy suddenly ran before them, waving his arms and shouting, "Freedom! Get the dogs!"

The firemen turned on the hoses full blast. The water pressure pinned a group of Negro girls against a wall. Police dogs tore at the demonstrators. The hoses swung around again; one jet was so powerful it peeled the bark from an elm tree.

On the sidelines, burly Negro steelworkers broke through the police lines and began to hurl rocks and bottles at the police. Reverend Fred J. Shuttlesworth, one of the movement's leaders, pleaded, "Get back, you are not helping our cause," but nobody listened.

The following day, crowds of enraged Negroes almost broke through the police barricades that separated the white and Negro sections of town. Dr. King, seeing that the situation was out of hand, called off the demonstrations for several days.

But there was no halt. Within a day or two demonstrations resumed. The Justice Department sent mediators, including Burke Marshall, Assistant Attorney General in charge of civil rights, to bring about a truce.

The truce, arranged by weary local and civil rights leaders at four o'clock in the morning, lasted only two days.

When night fell on May 11, 1963, one thousand white-robed Ku Klux Klansmen gathered for a rally in a park in nearby Bessemer. They lighted wooden crosses, and standing in the eerie light, leaders made racist speeches late into the night. Shortly before midnight, a car sped by the home of the Reverend A. D. King, Martin Luther King's younger brother. A bomb was thrown toward the front of the house. Reverend King and his children escaped unharmed through the back door as a second, more violent explosion rocked the house.

A few hours later, the Gaston Motel, where Martin Luther King and his assistants were staying, was bombed. Four people were injured, not seriously, and Dr. King escaped unhurt.

The streets around the motel filled with angry Negroes. When the police arrived, they were pelted with rocks and bricks.

"We are your friends," the police shouted, but the Negroes only jeered.

Reverend Wyatt T. Walker, one of Dr. King's assistants, came out of the motel. He had tied a white handkerchief around his arm as a symbol of peace, and he carried an electric megaphone. "Please go home," he pleaded with the Negroes. "Ladies and gentlemen, will you cooperate by going to your homes?"

The riot lasted for four hours. In its aftermath, there was new tension. Dr. King was certain that the long-range agreement made between civil rights leaders and Birmingham's city officials following the riots would stand up. "I do not believe that the bombings were perpetuated or even sanctioned by the majority of the white people in Birmingham," he said.

When agreement was finally reached and a biracial council was established to work out its details, Birmingham could be called a victory for the civil rights movement. Most of Dr. King's original demands had been met. But the price was heavy. And farther South, the price would be even heavier.

Medgar Evers, a slim, soft-spoken young NAACP official, believed that his life was in danger. The campaign of demonstrations that he was leading in Jackson, Mississippi, had encountered trouble from the Ku Klux Klan and other segregationist groups from the start. Evers's house was bombed, he was beaten, and his children's lives were threatened.

But his death on June 12,—at the hands of a sniper hiding in a honeysuckle thicket outside the Evers home—horrified even those who had opposed his work. The mayor wrote, "I am sick at heart," and put up a $5,000 reward for information leading to the arrest and conviction of Evers's killer.

During the next few days, the streets of Jackson filled with Negro demonstrators. Violence broke out several times. On the day of the funeral, Mayor Thompson lifted the ban on parades to permit the procession. It must be a silent march, he stipulated. The militant young Negroes were in no mood to obey that order.

At a signal, several hundred Negro youngsters surged forward. The angry crowd swelled to one thousand as the young people shouted, "We want the killer! We want the killer!" The police rushed forward, and in minutes a riot began.

At that moment, a tall, blond, young United States Justice Department lawyer named John Doar walked through the lines of police, past the barrage of rocks and bottles, into the center of the mob. "Medgar Evers wouldn't want it this way," he told the Negroes. "There are a lot of people in the United States pulling for you, but you can't do it with rocks, and bottles. . . . Hold hands with me and help us move these people along."

The crowd's fury died down; two Negroes joined hands with John Doar, and slowly the mob scattered.

All across America, people became increasingly aware of the electric quality of the Negro revolution. Most Americans were shocked by the pictures of Birmingham's police dogs, jaws open, lunging at demonstrators; at the story of William Moore, killed by a passing sniper; and at Medgar Evers's tragic death.

But as the demonstrations spread, some leaving tragedy in their wake, many Americans wondered whether the Negroes were not bringing this trouble on themselves. Why, they asked, were Negroes in such a hurry? Why couldn't they understand that change takes time? Why couldn't they wait?

But behind the Negro revolution were three centuries of waiting. Negroes felt that they had endured second-class citizenship all too long.

President Kennedy made it clear that he did indeed intend to keep the promises of first-class citizenship made to the Negroes by the Fourteenth Amendment nearly a hundred years earlier. In June, he made a nationwide television address. Speaking with deep emotion, he said:

"If an American, because his skin is dark, cannot eat lunch in a restaurant open to the public; if he cannot send his children to the best public school available; if he cannot vote for the public officials who represent him; if, in short, he cannot enjoy the full and free life which all of us want, then who among us would be content to have the color of his skin changed and stand in his place? . . .

"Are we to say to the world—and much more importantly, to each other—that this is the land of the free, *except for the Negroes;* that we have no second-class citizens, *except for the Negroes;* that we have no class or caste system, no ghettos, no master race, *except with respect to the Negroes?* . . . This nation, for all its hopes and boasts, will not be free until all its citizens are free. . . ."

A week later, President Kennedy sent to Congress the strongest civil rights legislation in American history. The bill asked for an end to segregation in hotels, restaurants, theaters, and all other public places. It outlawed discrimination in any state program which used federal funds. It called for the elimination of prejudice in labor unions and employment. Finally, it gave the Justice Department the power to bring suit against school districts where integration had not taken place.

In the past, civil rights legislation had been watered down by compromise. In 1957, a few congressmen had set up cots in the anterooms of Congress and taken turns talking all night, until they had diluted the law President Eisenhower had requested.

Now Negroes would march to Washington—to the very steps of the Capitol—to urge passage of the bill.

The largest "peaceful assembly to petition the government for a redress of grievances" that America had ever seen began at eight o'clock in the morning of August 28, 1963. The people who planned the "March on Washington" had hoped for a turnout of a hundred thousand people—but more than a quarter of a million came!

Here were Rosa Parks, the Montgomery seamstress whose arrest triggered the bus boycott and thus launched the nonviolent movement; Roy Wilkins, executive director of the NAACP; and young John Lewis, veteran freedom ride volunteer and the head of SNCC.

Here were Whitney Young, head of the National Urban League; A. Philip Randolph, the distinguished head of the Brotherhood of Sleeping Car Porters, who was one of the first planners of the demonstration; and Bayard Rustin, who had organized the giant rally. Missing, however, was James Farmer of CORE.

He was in a Louisiana jail, for taking part in a demonstration.

Students came from New York, Chicago, and Seattle. Negroes came from the Deep South clad in overalls. There were black-habited nuns and hundreds of priests and ministers and rabbis.

They came by bus, by train, by car, by plane. They hitchhiked from places as far away as California. Twelve young people walked from Brooklyn, New York, with knapsacks on their backs.

All morning the crowd grew—workers and businessmen, teachers, lawyers, children, housewives— black and white together.

They sang freedom songs, hands locked together, swaying to the rhythm:

> *"We shall overcome,*
> *We shall overcome,*
> *We shall overcome some day;*
> *Oh, deep in my heart, I do believe,*
> *We shall overcome some day;*

The leaders of the march separated from the crowd and went to the White House to meet with President Kennedy. There they heard him praise "the deep fervor and quiet dignity" of the marchers. "The nation," he said, "can properly be proud of the demonstration that has occurred here today."

But for the marchers, the high point of the day was the last speech—the one many of them had been waiting for—the address by Martin Luther King.

There, before the statue of Abraham Lincoln, he spoke words that might have been written by the gentle, brooding man from Illinois who envisioned an America united in bonds of brotherhood:

"Even though we face the difficulties of today and tomorrow, I still have a dream.

"It is a dream chiefly rooted in the American dream.

". . . that one day this nation will rise up and live out the true meaning of its creed 'We hold these truths to be self-evident, that all men are created equal.'

". . . that one day on the red hills of Georgia, the sons of former slaves and the sons of former slave owners will be able to sit together at the table of brotherhood. . . .

"I have a dream that my four little children will one day live in a nation where they will not be judged by the color of their skin, but by their . . . character. . . .

"Go back home," he told the marchers. "Go back to Alabama. Go back to Georgia. Go back to Louisiana. Go back to the Northern cities, to the slums, knowing that somehow this situation can and will be changed. Free at last, free at last. Thank God Almighty."

After they left, the melody of their songs and the sound of their marching feet echoed through Washington, through the halls of Congress, where the civil rights bill waited.

John Fitzgerald Kennedy did not live to see his bill

become law. It was still being debated in Congress when he was shot and killed in Dallas, Texas, in November of that year.

But Lyndon Baines Johnson carried on President Kennedy's commitment to the bill. In his first speech as the new President, he told a mourning Congress: "We have talked for 100 years or more. It is time to write the next chapter into the book of law. The need is *now.*"

It took the United States Senate and the House of Representatives almost a year to debate the law. In the past, Southern senators had been able to "filibuster," or "talk to death," any strong civil rights legislation, and once again they managed to delay the vote, for eighty-three days.

In order to stop a filibuster, two-thirds of the Senate must vote for "cloture"—a motion to end the debate on a resolution and take it to the floor for a vote. The filibuster is one of the oldest customs in the Senate, and never before had senators invoked cloture in a civil rights debate. But now, most of them felt strongly enough about the need for the new bill to break with tradition.

Speaking in favor of cloture, Senator Hubert Humphrey of Minnesota said: "The Constitution of the United States is on trial. The question is whether we will have two types of citizenship in this nation, or first-class citizenship for all." After that, the Senate voted to end the debate.

When the vote on the civil rights bill was taken,

the first Senator to vote was George Aiken of Vermont. "Mr. Aiken," the clerk called. The Senator stood up. "Aye," he said.

The roll call continued through the alphabet. When the votes were counted, the bill had drawn 73 ayes and only 27 nays. The Senate passed the bill on June 19, a year from the day President Kennedy had proposed the law.

Just before signing the bill, President Johnson spoke to the American people on television, to tell them about it:

"We believe that all men are created equal—yet many are denied equal treatment.

"We believe that all men have certain unalienable rights—yet many Americans do not enjoy those rights.

"We believe that all men are entitled to the blessings of liberty—yet millions are deprived of those blessings because of the color of their skin.

"The reasons are deeply imbedded in history and tradition and the nature of man. We can understand how this happened. But it cannot continue.

"Our Constitution, the foundation of our Republic, forbids it. The principles of our freedom forbid it. Morality forbids it. And the law I will sign tonight forbids it."

On July 2, 1964, in a room crowded with jubilant civil rights leaders, including Martin Luther King, President Johnson signed the new bill into law.

8 *The Long Walk to the Polls— the Mississippi Project*

It had been a revolutionary decade—those ten years between the May morning in 1954 when the nine judges of the Supreme Court ruled that segregating Negro children in school "may affect their minds and hearts in a way unlikely to ever be undone," and the July afternoon when President Johnson signed the Civil Rights Act of 1964—the act which in his words made "those who are equal before God now equal in the polling booths, in the classrooms, in the factories, and in hotels and restaurants and movie theaters and other places that provide service to the public."

Unlike other revolutions, this civil rights revolution did not want to overthrow a government. Rather, its goal was to guarantee a fair share of the blessings of democracy to the country's twenty million Negroes.

102

By 1964, much of that goal had been realized. In most of the nation, "white" and "colored" signs had all but vanished. Each September, white and Negro children went off to schools which previously had been segregated. Some states in the North and on the border of the South had new laws to outlaw discrimination in jobs and housing.

In the Deep South, it scarcely mattered that now many Negroes could eat lunch at integrated counters. Many Negroes there did not have the price of a restaurant meal. And it did not matter that in some parts of the country Negroes were gaining an increasing voice in the government. Nearly all Negroes in the rural areas in the Deep South were disenfranchised, unable to vote. Only about one-fourth of all the Negroes in the entire South voted in 1960. And in some states, Mississippi, for example, only 5 percent went to the polls.

The Fifteenth Amendment to our Constitution states,

> *"The right of citizens of the United States to vote shall not be denied or abridged by the United States or any State on account of race, color, or previous condition of servitude [slavery]."*

And for a time after its passage in 1870, five years after the Civil War, it was truly enforced. Jubilant over their newly established citizenship, 700,000 Negroes went to the polls, to vote for both white and Negro representatives.

The results were impressive. Fifty former slaves who had learned to read and write took seats alongside white legislators in the South Carolina Legislature. In Louisiana, O. J. Dunn, a Negro, served as lieutenant governor, and there were thirty-two Negro state senators and representatives.

Altogether, between 1869 and 1876, there were fifteen Negroes in the United States Congress. Their achievements stand as a memorial to them. "They opened the ballot box and jury box to thousands of white men who had been debarred by lack of earthly possession," wrote historian Albion W. Tourgee. "They introduced home rule to the South. They abolished the whipping post and branding iron." According to Republican leader James C. Blaine, "They were, as a rule, studious, earnest, ambitious men, whose public conduct would be honorable to any race."

But this state of affairs did not last long. Louisiana invented Jim Crow, and by the turn of the century, less than 5,000 of the 130,000 Negro names remained on the state's voting register. Other Southern states followed suit.

There were a number of ways to keep Negroes from voting. First came the poll tax. Most Negroes, as well as poor white people, had all they could do to provide food and shelter for their families. They could not afford to pay for the privilege of voting.

Second, difficult literacy tests were used. The registrar was free to ask any questions and to pass or fail any applicant he pleased. A Negro might be asked, "How many bubbles are there in a bar of soap?" Or he might be required to interpret an obscure idea in the state constitution. Or he might be failed for writing his age in years, instead of in months, on the application blank.

Third, the South invented the "white primary." The primary elections were "private party affairs," officials declared, and therefore were not subject to the Constitution's rulings on public elections. Since the end of Reconstruction, when white men united under the banner of the Democratic party, the South had been solidly one-party. So denial of the right to vote in the primary was, in effect, denial of the right to vote.

Fourth, Southern states enacted "grandfather clauses"—which reserved the right to vote without a literacy test to anyone whose forbears had voted before the Civil War.

In 1915, the Supreme Court struck down Oklahoma's grandfather clause, but it was not until 1939 that the Supreme Court was able to nullify the law in all Southern states.

It took even longer—until 1944, in fact—for the federal government to outlaw the white primary. It was not until July 23, 1964, when the Twenty-fourth Amendment to the Constitution was passed, that the use of poll taxes in federal elections was banished. And poll taxes in state and local elections were not declared unconstitutional until 1966.

A white overseer in predominantly Negro Baker County, Georgia—where only a few Negroes were registered in 1963—spoke for diehard Southern segregationists when he said: "It doesn't make any difference what Congress and the Supreme Court *say* the law is. It won't matter here *this* generation!"

A Negro in the Deep South who attempted to register might lose his job or his credit. He might be beaten, have his house set on fire, or be killed. "I don't want my job cut off," one man explained. Another was more blunt. "I don't want my throat cut," he said.

In the early 1960s, the Mississippi countryside seemed unchanged since the days of slavery. Here, in the Delta, the rising summer sun burnished the fields of growing cotton as it always had, cast a red glow on the unpainted frame shanties and tar-paper shacks that dotted the land.

To the Negro families who lived in these shacks, the civil rights revolution was only a myth, to be spoken of in whispers when people met in church or in the general store.

Mississippi Negroes watched wistfully as the freedom buses rolled over the highways in 1961, but there was little they could do to become part of the movement that those buses represented. They could not change their position—they were too poor, too uneducated, and, since in many counties it was "always open season on Niggers and rabbits," they were too frightened. Help had to come from outside.

One of the riders of those freedom buses was Bob Moses, a twenty-five-year-old Negro schoolteacher from New York. In Cleveland, Mississippi, Bob met another civil rights worker, a calm, soft-spoken farmer named Amzie Moore. Together they dreamed of what would happen to Mississippi if Negroes could vote. And then, one afternoon, they sat down at a pine table in a farmhouse on the Delta and planned a campaign to free Mississippi's Negroes from a bondage that sometimes seemed as oppressive as slavery.

"We've got to get people who will put their bodies into the struggle," Moses said. By this he meant that he would need to recruit an army of "guerilla fighters" from outside Mississippi who would penetrate the rural areas where federal civil rights laws were generally ignored.

Sixteen young people, both white and Negro, responded. Bob Moses gave them instructions:

"You are not freedom riders," he told them. "Stay out of jail if you can. Your job is to strengthen local people. If you can leave behind you people who are stronger and more skilled than when you came, there will be a core to work with next year."

The first job was to gain the trust of Mississippi's Negroes. It would be hard work, Bob told the volunteers, to help the Negroes overcome their fears. Leaders—local people—had to be trained in nonviolence. Negroes had to be taught how to register and vote. Some would have to be trained for better jobs. The volunteers would have to man food-distribution centers, for one of the ways that segregationists exerted power was to stop welfare deliveries of food and clothing to the poverty-stricken sharecroppers.

To the original "sixteen cats"—as James Forman called them—who volunteered for this "Mississippi Summer Project," Mississippi was a shock. They were prepared to find hordes of eager Negro youngsters fired with the enthusiasm of the Greensboro sit-ins, or older folks as patiently dedicated to gaining their rights as the Montgomery marchers were. Instead they found apathy. Oppression had crushed the spirit of revolt in rural Mississippi's Negroes.

The volunteers began to make their own plans.

"We've got to set up our own school system," one worker said. "These young people have never learned about freedom. They've got to be taught their own worth."

"The people here can't register or vote unless we teach them to read and write," another said.

"All they do is hang around in joints," came from another volunteer. "We need to set up community centers where people can go."

The volunteers set up the community centers and the classes. They taught Negro children about their own forebears. They told them stories of Crispus Attucks, a Negro, who died opposing British soldiers in Boston, Massachusetts, before the American Revolution. They brought books about Negro history, about Harriet Tubman, "the Moses of her people," who brought hundreds of escaped slaves to the North on the Underground Railroad, about Frederick Douglass, about the other abolitionists. The children learned about the important contributions that Negro Americans had made to our country.

The volunteers went out in twos every morning and knocked on farmhouse doors. "We're here to help you vote," they said. They brought sample registration forms and showed people how to fill them out. They encouraged Negroes to try to register and to go back to the courthouse over and over again. Many finally became enrolled voters.

Each year the numbers of volunteers grew. In the fall of 1961 there were sixteen. By 1964, there were over one thousand.

They came from the Ivy League colleges in the North, from the great Midwestern universities, from Negro colleges in the South. They came from towns and cities all over America.

They went to live in the little farm shanties, in church basements. They set up cots and electric plates in empty stores. Some picked vegetables and "chopped" cotton for their keep. They rode mules over country roads because there was no money for gasoline. They knocked on doors for food. Sometimes they ate only one meal a day—late at night, so that they didn't have to go to bed hungry. And in spite of all this, most of them felt that they gained more than they gave up.

One volunteer wrote home to his family: "There are old men and women who have little money, and none to spare, who stop you as you are leaving the church and say, 'I've waited 80 years for you to come and I just have to give you this little bit to let you all know how much we appreciate you coming. I prays for your safety every night, son. God bless you all.' And then they move down the stone steps and disappear along the red clay road lined with tall green trees and houses tumbling down."

But prayers for safety were not enough. The churches that served as "freedom schools" were bombed. Snipers followed civil rights workers home at night. The frame shanties were targets for swiftly spreading gasoline fires.

The most shocking tragedy occurred in Philadelphia, Mississippi, on June 21, 1964.

James Chaney, a twenty-one-year-old Negro plasterer from Meridian, Mississippi; Michael Schwerner, a twenty-four-year-old white New Yorker who headed a local freedom school; and Andrew Goodman, a twenty-one-year-old white student from New

110

York's Queens College, were arrested on a minor traffic charge. They were taken to jail. The deputy sheriff released them a few hours later. He warned them to "get out of the state."

The young men had been expected back at the project center at 4 P.M. When they failed to appear late that evening, volunteers notified the FBI. A mounting fear grew among the volunteers. "We are afraid that they have been murdered," one volunteer wrote in a letter. "Under the circumstances, that is the only thing that could have happened to them."

The young people who were working on the voter registration project were heavyhearted. Rumors flew, but the segregationists insisted that no harm had come to the boys. Their disappearance was called "just another trick." Then, two days after the boys vanished, their station wagon was found, charred and half buried in a swamp.

The United States Navy and the Mississippi State Highway Patrol sent men to search for clues. At last, a witness "tipped" the FBI.

On August 3, FBI investigators left Jackson, Mississippi. Outside Philadelphia, their car turned off the road and cut through a newly tilled farm. There, buried under an earthen dam, were the bullet-ridden, brutally beaten bodies of Andrew Goodman, James Chaney, and Michael Schwerner.

The death of the three young men shook America. In countless cities, memorial services were held for the three martyrs. But in the Delta, the tragedy had a special sadness. The work of the Mississippi Project volunteers had enriched the lives of many of the people who lived there.

The civil rights revolutionaries no longer wore the suits and white shirts, the neat sweaters and skirts, of the college sit-ins. They now wore faded, dusty overalls and patched cotton dresses. The revolt had become a "grass-roots movement." New Negro leaders were emerging from the hamlets and cotton fields. These people, encouraged and trained by Mississippi Project volunteers, were now ready to take over the reins of the civil rights movement in the Delta.

Fannie Lou Hamer, a Negro sharecropper in Sunflower County, Mississippi, who was to become one of these new leaders, tells her story.

"I went to a meeting at this church in Ruleville. . . . James Bevel [a SNCC volunteer] did talk that night, and everything he said made sense. So when they stopped talking, they wanted to know who would go down to register, and I held up my hand.

"The thirty-first of August, in '62, the day I went into the courthouse to register, the man that I had worked for as a timekeeper and sharecropper for eighteen years, he said that I would have to leave."

After she lost her job, Mrs. Hamer went to stay with a friend in Ruleville. A few days later, a car packed with Ku Klux Klansmen drove past the house, and sixteen bullets were pumped into the bedroom

112

where she slept. She v   .t night, and no one was hurt.

On June 9, 1963, Mrs.   ested in Winona, Mississippi. While she v   .1, she was badly beaten with a blackjack. But   .r determination to work in the voter registration drive did not falter.

Sometimes the trip to the courthouse where the local board of registry met was filled with obstacles. Sometimes registrars would only register one or two Negroes a day. Other times they would put signs on the door that said, "Office is closed today."

Often it was all the volunteers could do to keep up the Negroes' courage. One young Negro girl made eight trips to the courthouse. Each time she was told, "Sorry, but you didn't pass the test." The eighth time, she returned to the Mississippi Project community center weeping.

"I just can't do it again," she sobbed.

"Try, just one more time," she was told.

The ninth time, she passed the test and became a registered voter!

Segregationists watched the list of Negro voters grow, a name or two at a time. "Most of those people wouldn't vote if they could," some scoffed.

When Mississippi Negroes found the voting booths firmly closed to them, the movement set up its own polling places, printed its own ballots, and ran its own candidates in mock elections called "freedom elections." Their purpose was to show that Negroes *would* vote in regular elections if the barriers were let down.

Out of these freedom elections—in which 85,000 Negroes voted, from a potential of 430,000—came the Freedom Democratic Party.

The Freedom Democratic Party was a protest, just as the sit-ins and the bus boycott had been. Negroes wanted a voice in the actual government of the United States. They wanted the right to vote and the right to elect representatives. "We are no longer fighting for a seat at the lunch counter," the Reverend James Bevel said. "We are fighting for seats in the Legislature."

As Negroes began to register in ever-increasing numbers, slowly changes began to take place. A Georgia Senator remarked in 1966, Negroes were becoming a potent force in government. "I don't think you will see any more race baiting in the future," he said. "I think that now all candidates are going to solicit the votes of *all* Georgia citizens."

The keys to the ballot box unlocked other doors, too. Negroes asked for laws to punish "night riders" —the vigilantes who committed racial crimes. Mississippi's Governor Johnson began a campaign to get stronger laws in "protecting the lives and property of *all* Mississippi citizens from the ravages of civil disorder."

Southern Negroes had long been the victims of unfair legal practices. On the one hand, crimes against Negroes rarely got to court; on the other hand, Negroes were never selected to serve on juries in cases where a white man was tried for a crime against a Negro. But in 1966, in Georgia, for the first time since Reconstruction, a predominantly Negro trial jury was selected; and in the same year, in Alabama, for the first time this century, the courts found a white man guilty of murdering a Negro.

In 1966, the federal government began to invoke a law passed in 1871, because there was no other way for the federal authorities to prosecute those who had murdered the three civil rights workers in Mississippi. Under this law, the government may bring a criminal charge of "interfering with persons' civil rights." Although the penalty for even such brutal crimes as the murders of Andrew Goodman, James Chaney, and Michael Schwerner is only one year in prison under this law, the very fact that the law will be used may discourage night riders; until the federal government is empowered to prosecute under new, more effective legislation.

At first, the Mississippi Project volunteers made little progress. But gradually, the list of names on the voting registers began to increase. In 1960, only about one-fourth of the Negroes in the South voted. By 1964, following the powerful stimulant given to the movement by the "new abolitionists," as the volunteers were called, 34 percent were registered. And by the spring of 1966, nearly half of the eligible Negro voters were registered.

° The Voting Rights Act of 1965 provided that in

counties where local registrars showed discrimination against Negroes, the federal government could send federally appointed examiners to man the registration booths. This was another reason why over one million new names were on the voting lists by the spring of 1966, and the way was open to register the remaining two million disenfranchised Negroes.

By the spring of 1966, America had taken sizable steps toward granting Negroes the protection guaranteed by the Fifteenth Amendment. The provisions of the Voting Rights Act of 1965, favorable decisions by the Supreme Court, and the vigorous enforcement of law by the Justice Department were all responsible for closing the old loopholes.

But it was the young people of the Mississippi Project who traveled deep into the South, leaving behind them their homes, friends, careers, and all thought of their own safety, who brought the beginnings of full citizenship to people for whom democracy had only been a dream.

9 *The Crisis Moves North*

Early one evening in the fall of 1963, a group of CORE pickets gathered in front of a hamburger stand on the outskirts of New York City. They marched slowly in front of the small white stucco building. Some carried signs demanding "Equal Opportunity in Employment"; others carried signs calling for "Jobs for Negroes, NOW"; all of them were singing:

> *"We'll walk hand in hand,*
> *We'll walk hand in hand,*
> *We'll walk hand in hand, some day,*
> *O, deep in my heart, I do believe,*
> *We shall overcome some day."*

117

Behind a police barricade, white hecklers catcalled and jeered. Parked at the curb were two police cars, and patrolmen walked back and forth, billy sticks in their hands, separating the pickets from the hoodlums.

Passersby looked curiously at the scene. "It's hard to believe this is New York," one said. "It looks like Birmingham."

As the civil rights movement grew in momentum and spread from the South into the North, the Midwest, and the West, people in these regions were surprised to find that Negroes in their own cities had so many grievances.

Southerners did not understand Negroes' complaints because they were convinced that "our Negroes are happy the way things are." Northerners were blind to racial inequality because they believed that "Negroes in the North already *have* equal rights."

It was true that above the old Mason-Dixon line, Negroes were given full *legal* rights. They could vote, and in fact, some communities had Negro representatives in government. There were no Jim Crow signs. Some states even had special laws forbidding discrimination in jobs and housing and in restaurants, theaters, schools, hotels, and other public places. But the law was one matter, the unwritten law was quite another matter.

Because more jobs were available in the North, a

Negro father was likely to come to New York or Detroit, Michigan, or Chicago in search of a good job. But, he usually was unable to find one. Many firms hired only white applicants. "Last to be hired, first to be fired" was often the Negro's lot in employment.

Even when an employer was willing to give a Negro an equal chance, he found it hard to find qualified Negroes. Many labor unions had discriminatory systems; they would not allow Negroes to become apprentices. In fact, in 1956, only one apprentice in a hundred was a Negro. Denied the opportunity to learn skills, many Negroes were unable to find good jobs. Twice as many Negroes were unemployed as were whites, and three times as many were "permanently unemployed"—that is, they were out of work for more than half a year at a time.

Others settled for menial jobs, as laborers or porters. In New York City's Harlem, which was typical of Negro ghettos throughout the North, twice as many men had low-paying unskilled jobs as did men who lived in other parts of the city.

Even well-educated Negroes did not reap the same rewards as did whites. In 1960, Negroes who had completed four years of college could expect to earn in their lifetime only as much as whites who had not gone beyond the eighth grade.

In Northern cities, the median family income for Negroes was only two-thirds as high as the median white-family income. Since the average Negro father could not provide enough money to support the family adequately, the average Negro mother, too, had her share of problems. She had to make a home for her husband and children in a run-down, often rat-infested slum. Like slums everywhere in the world, these areas had a high disease and crime rate.

Even if the family could afford to buy a decent house in a good neighborhood, there were few places to be had. White homeowners often made a "gentlemen's agreement" not to sell their houses to colored buyers. The sale of a home to a Negro family does not cause property values to fall, but panic does. When someone decides, "If a Negro family moves into the neighborhood, all the white people will move out, and it will become a Negro ghetto," their idea may be wrong, but it triggers a selling trend. And this in time causes prices to drop. So often, when a Negro purchases a house, his white neighbors quickly put "For Sale" signs on their homes and flee.

As the civil rights movement grew in some communities, public-spirited white people made it known that they would welcome Negro neighbors. They formed "fair housing" groups in order to help Negroes obtain homes in white areas. Even then, Negroes thought twice about moving in. They were afraid their children might find it difficult to make friends in the neighborhood.

For Negro children, the burden was hardest of all.

There was no legalized segregation in Northern schools, as there was in Southern schools—no laws forbidding white and Negro children to attend the same schools. But because schools take children from nearby neighborhoods, a school in an all-Negro neighborhood will be all-Negro, just as one in an all-white neighborhood will have only white students. Many schools in the North were just as segregated as those in the South.

All-Negro schools in the North, just as in the South, were usually inferior. They were generally housed in old, run-down buildings. Funds available for equipment and teachers were less than those for the white schools.

In 1954, when the Supreme Court decided that Linda Brown's "separate but equal" school was unconstitutional, many Northern Negro parents complained that the schools *their* children attended were illegal, too. But integrating Northern schools proved to be as difficult as integrating Southern schools.

Some Northern communities were able to solve the problem smoothly. Some, for example, closed the all-Negro schools, enlarged the remaining schools, and reassigned the Negro children to them. Some redistributed the children so that each school had a share of both white and Negro youngsters.

School boards in various communities tried different plans. Some built schools right on the borders of white and Negro neighborhoods, so that the schools would have students from each area. Some tried the "Princeton plan," in which children were assigned to schools according to grade, rather than neighborhood. Others experimented with centrally located school complexes, so that all of a particular community's schools, from kindergarten through high school, were built on one site.

But when school boards began to transfer children to schools outside of their own neighborhoods in order to have racially balanced schools, white parents often complained bitterly. They wanted their children to attend nearby schools. Wasn't the North doing, in reverse, what the South had done before the Supreme Court decision—that is, assigning children by *race?* After all, they said, wasn't Oliver Brown's complaint that Linda had to walk twenty-one blocks to school although there was another school right in her own neighborhood? Why should their own children have to walk—or ride a bus—to get to schools that were far away?

Some parents hoped to find the answers to these questions in the courts. But the courts had a difficult job in applying the verdict in Oliver Brown's case to schools in the North. The decision in *Brown v. Board of Education* speaks of "segregation *with the sanction of law.*" And so, in New Rochelle, New York, for example, the United States Federal District Court found that since the city had redrawn the boundaries of the school district solely in order to keep all the

Negro children in one school, the resulting segregation was a matter of *law*, and the *Brown v. Board of Education* decision held. The school board was ordered to desegregate the schools. But in other places, where segregation was simply a result of the racial makeup of the town rather than the result of a deliberate plan, the courts disagreed over whether school boards had to end the segregation.

Harold Howe, United States Commissioner of Education described the difficulties of "whittling away at segregation" in the North. "Segregation in the North," he said, was "caused by a wide variety of reasons . . . but most of all [it comes] from the subtle influence of prejudice which herds the Negro into the city ghetto. These influences are outside of the law, but they operate as effectively as legal separation ever did in the South. While progress is being made in enforcing the law against school segregation in the South, efforts to end segregation in the North are bogged down in quicksands of legal interpretation."

With no clear-cut guidelines, parents and school boards frequently became locked in argument. Again and again, people took to the streets to demonstrate. One spectacular demonstration took place in New York City, in February, 1964, when Negro parents staged a giant school boycott. Nearly half a million children stayed home. But even so, the difficult problems of transporting pupils in a large city made real integration nearly impossible.

Other boycotts, too, became part of the changing scene in the North. In New York and Philadelphia, pickets encircled the offices of a dairy company, carrying signs that said, "Equal Employment Opportunity for Everyone." CORE organized the demonstration, and other groups, including some labor unions, sent pickets to march along with the CORE demonstrators.

Factories, construction sites, and stores were picketed by demonstrators who demanded that Negroes be hired on an equal basis. While the New York World's Fair was being built, during 1963 and 1964, pickets demanded that labor unions and businesses use Negro labor, and on April 22, 1964, demonstrators drowned out President Johnson's speech at the World's Fair with their chants: "End Jim Crow! Equal jobs for all!"

Discrimination in housing, too, was under fire. In New York's Negro section, Harlem, slum residents went on "rent strikes." They refused to pay their rents until landlords repaired broken windows, faulty plumbing and heating facilities, and dangerous ill-lighted staircases.

Militant Negro groups called for "stall-ins," to halt traffic, and thus focus attention on the Negro problem. One day, they blocked off the entrances and exits to Jones Beach State Park on Long Island, keeping thousands of sweltering people from reaching the beach.

Many white people in the North were sympathetic

to the Negroes' struggle as it unfolded in Little Rock and in Montgomery. But when people were faced with demonstrations in their own neighborhoods, resentment against Negroes grew strong. This anger—the "white backlash"—even became a campaign issue during the presidential election of 1964.

A Negro civil rights leader explained the cause of the backlash. "Lots of white people think we are trying to take something *away* from them. They don't understand that all we want is our fair share of the privileges that whites already enjoy."

Some Negroes thought that the civil rights movement was too mild a solution to their problems. All around them they saw filthy slums, ill-kept segregated schools, poverty, and disease. Their frustrations mounted. Integration would never work, they decided. And in desperation, they turned toward Negro segregationist groups such as the Nation of Islam—the Black Muslims—just as some Negroes of an earlier generation had turned toward Marcus Garvey's brand of Black Nationalism, and still farther back in time, some had supported the "Back to Africa" movements of the nineteenth century.

W. D. Fard rallied the Black Muslims in Detroit in 1930. His chief lieutenant, Elijah Muhammed, a soft-spoken Chicagoan with a mysterious past, gave the movement real impetus. In turn, Muhammed's disciple, Malcom X, became the Muslims' chief spokesman.

Malcolm X taught his followers to discard their last

names and use letters and numbers instead. The reason was that Negro slaves had been given their masters' surnames and these last names were now a reminder of slavery.

Like other Black Nationalist leaders before him, Malcolm X told Negroes, "Be proud of your black skin." He told Negroes that they could succeed only by helping themselves. He preached a program of thrift, honesty, cleanliness, and self-discipline. He told his people to avoid liquor, tobacco, and drugs.

Malcolm X was a fiery and convincing speaker. He understood the resentments of Negroes in Northern cities, for he was a product of the ghetto. He had lived in the underworld, and he spoke with authority about the tragedy and terror of life in the slums. Even Negroes who did not believe in the Muslims' goals of separation of the races thought that Malcolm X's bleak picture of Negro life in America was true. Although the Muslims' membership rolls were small, Malcolm X's voice was a stirring one.

In 1964, Malcolm X split with the Muslims and set up his own movement, the Organization of Afro-American Unity. The argument between his group and its parent organization grew more and more heated. A year later, as he was preparing to address an audience of his followers, he was shot. Among the three men convicted of the crime were two Black Muslims.

If the Black Muslim movement, with its orders to

"fight violence with violence," did not have the solution to the problems of Negroes in Northern cities, neither did the civil rights movement, some Negroes argued. To take Negro children out of the vicious cycle—slum homes, poor schools, menial jobs or no jobs at all—would require major changes. And these changes were slow in coming. Meanwhile, civil rights leaders warned that Negroes' frustrations were reaching a boiling point.

By the summer of 1964, the mood in Harlem, New York's ghetto, was tense. Gone was the cheerful, optimistic spirit of the March on Washington of the previous year. Street gangs stalked the crowded slums; idle men and women sat on steps; children with no place to go and nothing to do played restlessly on the steamy city streets and garbage-littered lots.

In August, Harlem was a bomb that was ready to explode. The blast was set off when a young Negro boy, on his way home from summer school, got into a fight with another youngster. During the fight, an off-duty policeman shot and killed the boy.

Although a grand jury investigating the case later decided that the policeman had acted in self-defense, Harlem's Negroes saw the tragedy as another example of the "police brutality" they feared so much.

The day after the boy's death, a CORE rally was held. The streets filled with thousands of angry mourners.

"We asked for civil rights," a young girl shouted

from her seat on a hastily built platform, "and we got white backlash and a dead boy."

Riots broke out late that night. Screaming mobs of Negroes swarmed through Harlem, looting stores, breaking windows, overturning cars, and fighting the hundreds of policemen who had sped to the scene. They climbed to the tops of the tenement buildings and showered the policemen with bottles, bricks, and debris.

On one corner, a policeman shouted to the crowd through a bullhorn, "Go home, go home."

"We *are* home, baby," a man in the crowd answered him.

Police fired volleys of bullets in the air to disperse the mob. At last, at dawn, the riot was spent.

But the disaster in Harlem was only one of many. Outbreaks of violence occurred in Philadelphia, in Rochester, New York, in Jersey City, New Jersey, in the Bedford-Stuyvesant section of Brooklyn.

The worst came a year later, in Watts, the Negro slum of Los Angeles.

Watts does not look like the Negro slums of New York, Chicago, or Detroit. Here, instead of decaying tenements packed close to one another on the gritty streets, the houses are one-story, pastel stucco buildings. Some are set back from the street and surrounded by small patches of grass. Here and there are palm trees and pretty yucca plants.

But appearances are sometimes deceiving. The Negroes who lived in Watts face the same seemingly unsolvable problems that are found in Negro slums all over America.

A constant migration of underprivileged Negroes, unable to work in the South because of increased automation on the farms, floods Watts each year with a highly illiterate population. All the other by-products of poverty and discrimination, too, haunt Watts: low wages, mass unemployment, inferior schools.

The fact that Los Angeles is spread over a large area and that there is no effective public transportation system to connect Watts to the rest of the city aggravates the problems of Watts.

"You can get out of Harlem if you have 15 cents for a subway ride," one civil rights worker said. "But in Watts you are trapped in the ghetto."

The civil rights movement had made no inroads in Los Angeles. Martin Luther King had said, some years before, "It is going to be much harder to have a civil rights movement in the cities of the North than in the South," and it was certainly true in Los Angeles.

Then, too, the civil rights cause had suffered serious setbacks in California. The California fair housing laws—the legislation that made it possible for Negroes to get out of the ghettos by buying or renting homes in white neighborhoods—had been repealed, in November of 1964.

Los Angeles, alone among all the major cities outside the South, had no local organization to fight unemployment and illiteracy under the federal antipoverty program.

And, perhaps most important, Negroes resented Los Angeles Police Chief William Parker. Chief Parker, who ran a modern and efficient police department, had been quoted as saying that the Supreme Court Decision of 1954 was "legal idealism." He also had said that he thought the civil rights movement was a "social danger."

As in New York, it was a clash between the police and some local Negroes that set off the Watts riots of 1965. A man was arrested on a charge of reckless driving. Several people began to argue with the officer who gave the ticket. The story spread, and angry crowds began to form on street corners.

Within a few hours, marauding bands roamed the city, looting, burning houses and stores. Instead of bricks and bottles, guns and "Molotov cocktails"— bottles of gasoline with wicks—were used as weapons. "They've got weapons and ammo," one of the twenty thousand National Guardsmen who were called in said. "It's going to be like Vietnam."

The three-thousand-square-block area of Watts did, indeed, look like a war-torn city. National Guardsmen, with fixed bayonets and machine guns, received reinforcements by helicopter and jeeps. On block after block, houses and stores were totally demolished. Residents took cover, only to have to flee from the spreading flames.

Here and there, Negro store owners tried to save their property. "Blood Brother," the signs on the windows said, or "Negro owned and operated. We shall overcome."

But the signs did little good. In the Watts riots, violence was not directed specifically against whites. The destruction was confined to the Negro ghetto. Seeing no way out of their frustrations and being without effective leadership to direct their anger constructively, the rioters in Watts simply struck out blindly, destroying what was close at hand.

Many escaped into other neighborhoods. Some took other refugees with them. Bishop R. J. Morris, a Methodist minister, ignored angry threats from other Negroes when he rescued a teen-age white couple whose car was caught in the cross fire.

"Go back to your church," one rioter warned.

"I'm going to help these young people," the minister replied. He drove away with them in his car.

But many were not so lucky, and for them there was no escape. In the tragic aftermath, thirty-three were found dead. One, a deputy sheriff, had been shot by rioters. Twenty-six were killed by police. The others died in fires and other accidents.

President Johnson moved swiftly during the Watts crisis. He sent two key administration officials to meet with California's Governor "Pat" Brown and find a solution.

The American people were baffled and angry about the riots. President Johnson spoke on national television to explain the reasons for the outbursts.

"The bitter years that preceded the riots, the death of hope, where hope existed, [and] the sense of failure to change the conditions of life lead to these riots. *But they do not justify them.*"

The Civil Rights revolution, the President said, was made up of "brilliant promises and stunning reverses." He asked for understanding and tolerance. He called upon the American people to help "equip the poor and oppressed for the long march to dignity and well-being."

Afterward, the McCone Commission, appointed to investigate the Watts riots, warned that Watts was "only a curtain raiser" for future violence, unless an all-out attack was made on the causes of discontent in the Northern cities.

First, it suggested, adults who could not read and write well enough to fill out job forms or read instructions should be offered emergency schooling. Job training, too, was necessary, to give unskilled adults the means to fill jobs in today's technological society.

The slums, breeding ground of crime, must be replaced with adequate housing.

The last suggestion the commission made was for the city to set up a panel made up of local people who would work to bring about trust and friendship between the police and the people.

The McCone Commission's findings put the problems of the Northern cities into clearer focus. By the middle of the 1960s it was evident that changes in the law would accomplish little, for many Northern states already had civil rights laws—fair employment practices laws and laws making it a crime to refuse to sell or rent houses to Negroes. These laws went beyond federal legislation. The problems in Northern cities were economic and social, rather than legal, and they were beyond the reach of civil rights laws. They called for broader, more drastic remedies—remedies that would help people, as the McCone Commission suggested, "pull themselves up by their bootstraps." And these programs would have to be instituted by the federal government, assisted by state and local governments.

On November 5, 1964, as the first stepping-stones on the "long march to dignity and well-being," the federal government allotted 1 billion dollars to the new Office of Economic Opportunity. The program was not limited to Negroes. But because Negroes make up the bottom rung of the economic ladder in the United States, the program was designed to help them in their specific problems.

The Job Corps gives education and job training to young people between the ages of sixteen and twenty-one who are out of school and out of work. At its

133

camps, young people can live, work, and learn. For those who choose to stay in their own cities, the Neighborhood Youth Corps provides part-time or full-time work. These jobs are in hospitals, settlement houses, schools, libraries, courts of law, and parks and playgrounds.

The College Work Study Program assists bright students from low-income families by offering them jobs to help pay for their tuition and living expenses.

For men and women trapped by a lack of education, the Adult Basic Education Program offers swift-paced "catch-up" classes. There is also the Work Experience Program to teach new skills to adults who lack the skills to compete for good jobs.

And perhaps most important, there are programs that will give underprivileged children a chance to begin primary school without the disadvantages slum children usually have. In Operation Headstart, preschool children are given a "boost" to help them catch up in speech and other skills, for without special training, children who have never had toys or crayons or pencils or books, and who have never been taken to museums or zoos, cannot achieve as well in school as can more fortunate children.

As Negroes, in ever-larger numbers, leave the farms and hamlets of the South for a new life in Northern cities, the role of Negro Americans becomes increasingly tied in with the special problems of today's cities. When the need arose for a special department in the federal government to handle city affairs, President Johnson appointed Robert C. Weaver to head the Department of Housing and Urban Development. Secretary Weaver became the first Negro in history to serve as a member of a President's cabinet.

Early in 1966, President Johnson appointed Roger W. Wilkins to head the United States Community Relations Service. The new director, who is a nephew of NAACP President Roy Wilkins, is a "troubleshooter"; his task is to root out the causes of trouble in the Northern cities.

"Our main job," he explained, "is to keep our fingers on the pulse of the ghetto and to build progress people can *see and feel.*"

Since the civil rights revolution began, there has been much progress that people can see and feel. In the South, where Jim Crow was always visible, the changes have been dramatic. In the North, where discrimination took a more subtle shape, many changes are still unseen.

The problems of the Negroes in the North continue to be serious. High unemployment, lack of education, bad housing, crime, and disease still blight the big Northern cities. Nor are major changes likely to come soon, for the programs that are directed to these problems are as yet small in scope and still mainly in the experimental phase.

In the spring of 1966, an important Civil Rights conference was held in the White House. As a result of the meeting of nearly two thousand delegates from different walks of life, a report was submitted to President Johnson which contained recommendations for federal action. These included huge public works programs, increased funds for antipoverty programs, guaranteed jobs or income for every family, and large new outlays for education. These programs were planned mainly for the North and were aimed at helping "American Negroes achieve in reality the rights that have been opened to them in theory."

10 To Fulfill the Promise of America

Spread on the President's desk—some said it was the very desk on which Abraham Lincoln signed the Emancipation Proclamation—was a sheaf of official papers. Pen in hand, President Lyndon Johnson paused to look over the documents quickly, for he knew very well what they contained.

The final draft of the Voting Rights Act of 1965 was ready. A stroke of the President's pen would give the federal government broad new powers to enforce the Fifteenth Amendment—the section of the Constitution that guarantees the right to vote to every American citizen, regardless of his race or color.

The Voting Rights Act of 1965 was the culmination of a series of laws that were, as President Johnson said, to extend "the promise of America [so] that

137

every person shall share in the blessings of this land."
This law, like the others in the recent past, was really
a part of the unfinished business of the Civil War.
When the Emancipation Proclamation was signed,
more than a century earlier, and the Negro began the
journey that took him from slavery to citizenship, it
was the responsibility of our nation to grant him the
same kind of citizenship that it bestowed upon every
other American.

American citizenship was, in the words of George
Washington, "the sweet enjoyment of the benign influence of good laws under a free government." What
a wide spectrum of rights, duties, and privileges these
words invoke!

The "good laws" of the Bill of Rights included
freedom of religion, of speech, and of the press; and
the right of the people peaceably to assemble and to
petition the government for a redress of grievances.

They included the right to full justice under the
law: the right to be secure against unreasonable
searches and seizures; the right to a speedy and public trial, by an impartial jury; the right to be confronted with the nature of an accusation and with
one's accusers; the right to counsel for defense; the
right not to be compelled to testify against oneself;
and the right not to be deprived of life, liberty, and
property without due process of law.

And there was the right to vote, to have a voice in
making and enforcing those "good laws under a free

government"—a right that, as later amendments over the years ensured, was not to be restricted or denied because of race, color, or sex.

These are some of the basic tenets of American citizenship. After the Civil War, they were granted to the Negro. The Thirteenth Amendment, in freeing him, left him in a limbo between slavery and citizenship. The Fourteenth Amendment made his position plain. He was to be nothing less than a full citizen by virtue of the fact that "all persons born or naturalized in the United States . . . are citizens of the United States." Furthermore, these citizenship rights were not to be limited in any way, for the amendment continued, "No state shall make or enforce any law which shall abridge the privileges or immunities of citizens of the United States."

With the Negro's status as a citizen clearly established, the nation went on to the next step, the right to vote guaranteed in the Fifteenth Amendment. This right was not to be "denied or abridged by the United States or by any State on account of race, color, or previous condition of servitude."

When the South returned to home rule in 1877, the nation gradually neglected the guarantees of civic and political equality that it had made to Negroes. But the challenge, evaded for nearly a century, was not to be ignored forever. In the middle of the twentieth century, the nation was again brought to a confrontation.

In 1954, the Supreme Court exposed the contradiction in our democracy that America for so long had swept under the rug. Legal grounds for segregation —and for the second-class citizenship that segregation established—were destroyed. But the Court's decision lacked teeth. The Supreme Court is a judicial body—it can only make judgments on the basis of the existing laws. The nation needed new laws to spell out the government's responsibility in civil rights and to provide legal guidelines for behavior.

The first of these new laws, the Civil Rights Act of 1957, was originally designed to enforce school desegregation. In its first draft, it gave the Justice Department power to bring suit on behalf of any civil rights violation, including school segregation and denial of the vote. The school provision was dropped, but in its final form, the act created a Commission on Civil Rights. The Commission could investigate the denial of voting rights based on unfair (racial) discrimination. The act also gave the Department of Justice some limited powers of enforcement.

The Civil Rights Act of 1957 really did little more than point out the loopholes by which states had been able to keep Negroes from voting. But, it paved the way for the laws in the next few years to seal these loopholes.

The Twenty-fourth Amendment to the Constitution, ratified in 1964, ended the poll tax in federal elections. The 1960 Civil Rights Act gave the Justice

140

Department the right to examine states' voting records and to decide whether communities were using devious methods to keep Negroes from voting. It also provided criminal penalties for bombing and mob action to obstruct court orders.

Early in 1963, President Kennedy sent a relatively mild civil rights bill to Congress. But as he said later, "the events in Birmingham and elsewhere" had convinced him that the matter was urgent. On June 11, he addressed the nation. "The fires of frustration and discord are burning in every city, North and South," he said. "Where legal remedies are not at hand, redress is sought in the streets in demonstrations, parades and protests, which create tensions and threaten violence—and threaten lives." He outlined much stronger legal remedies in his new bill, and urged it be passed—"above all because it is *right*."

The Civil Rights Act of 1964, passed after President Kennedy's death, outlawed discrimination in any state program receiving federal aid. It outlawed racial barriers in employment, in labor union membership. It gave further enforcement powers against discrimination in voting. It enabled the Justice Department to bring suit for desegregation of schools. And it crumbled still other barriers Jim Crow had built, by prohibiting segregation in parks, restaurants, libraries, hotels, railroad, and bus terminals—in every place that serves the public.

The new civil rights laws brought increasing numbers of Negroes to the polls. There were 450,000 new Negro voters registered in the South between 1954 and 1965, and 1 million more by 1966, and hundreds of thousands more are expected to be added as the Voting Rights Act of 1965 becomes better enforced.

The Negroes' new political status during this decade was shown by the appointment of many federal officials. Eight Negroes were named federal judges, and four were made United States ambassadors. Thurgood Marshall was appointed Solicitor General, and Robert C. Weaver was given a Cabinet position. Negro candidates captured more than 280 election offices. They won six seats in Congress and more than ninety in state legislatures, including several in the South.

But life in America is more than a matter of laws on the books. It is more than a free ballot and the right to use public facilities. Everyday life in our country is also a matter of the kind of a job a person may hold, the kind of education a child may receive, and where and how families live. Here, Negroes scored more gains in the short years between 1955 and 1965 than in any period in American history.

As historian C. Vann Woodward pointed out, these gains could be measured in savings accounts, insurance policies, and purchasing power, in high school and college diplomas. They could be measured also in new opportunities for those who qualified for professional and clerical jobs.

But impressive as these gains are, it was a small number of Negroes who benefited, in the main. For the majority of Negroes, now living in the increasingly ghettoized cities outside of the South, the past ten years have brought little change. Each year, although a greater number of previously all-white schools throughout the country become integrated, the continued migration of Negroes from the South brings more Negro children into the ghetto schools.

For many, the civil rights movement served to show the large gaps in employment, income, education, and housing that exist between Negroes and whites. Many Negroes became convinced that they must have "bargaining power" in order to close these gaps. Dr. Martin Luther King explained this aim, when he said, in 1966, "Negroes have to acquire a *share of power* so that they may act in their own interests as an independent social force."

The question of just what this power was to be and how it was to be obtained began to cause splits in Negro leadership and among Negro citizens in general. SNCC, CORE, the NAACP, the SCLC, and other groups differed in their interpretations of what "bargaining power" meant. To some, it meant that Negroes had to seek additional voting power, sometimes independent of the existing parties. To others, it meant modifying the principles of nonviolence that had been the earlier effective method of the civil rights movement.

Some thought that it was most important for Negroes who had been accustomed to accepting themselves as second-class citizens to create a proud new self-image by accomplishing major gains on their own, completely through their own efforts.

There were many differences of opinion about new directions in the civil rights movement and the question of Negro-white unity after 1965. But Dr. King spoke for the vast majority when he said, "Negroes want to share power to bring about a community in which neither power nor dignity will be colored black or white."

As it entered its second decade, the civil rights movement could look back on a stormy past and ahead to a future in which many problems remain unsolved. White backlash erupted with unexpected fury in many Northern cities in the summer of 1966, and new riots broke out again among Negroes in the ghettos.

But despite the delays and disappointments, the civil rights movement has dramatically changed our country. Negro youngsters today are growing up in a nation that is very different from the nation in which their parents and grandparents were children. But what about the nine out of ten Americans who are not Negro? What do the important changes of the past decade mean in terms of the kind of a nation all Americans believe in?

To find the answer to that question, we have to ask ourselves, "What does democracy actually mean?"

Perhaps we can answer, with President John F. Kennedy, "True democracy, living and growing and inspiring, puts its faith in the people—faith that the people will reward courage, respect honor, and ultimately recognize right."

"That the people will reward courage, respect honor, and ultimately recognize right!" How many Americans in the past few years have staked their hopes, and even their lives, on that belief! Among their ranks were:

Oliver Brown, whose protests against his little daughter Linda's being made to attend a segregated school helped to end the doctrine of "separate but equal" in public education.

Chief Justice Earl Warren, spokesman for his colleagues in the Supreme Court, whose belief in a color-blind Constitution helped create the climate for a change in American justice.

Martin Luther King, who told his people, "To the degree that I harm my brother, no matter what he is doing to me, to that extent, I harm myself."

The old woman who trudged wearily to work during the Montgomery bus boycott and refused the offer of a ride by saying, "I'm not walking for myself —I'm walking for my children and my grandchildren."

The Negro boy who walked to school, past jeering white crowds, with this determination: "As long as I can walk, I'm going to that school."

The "new abolitionists"—the young people of the

Mississippi Project—who went deep into the South to "melt the iceberg of segregation."

The children of Birmingham, who marched during the day and filled the overflowing jails at night.

The clergymen, of all races and creeds, who locked hands together to sing "We Shall Overcome" at the foot of the Lincoln Memorial.

And the martyrs—more than twenty-five of them, white and Negro—whose lives testify to their belief in the brotherhood of men.

And there were more, too, many more, unnamed and unknown, who, by taking part in the civil rights struggle, put their stamp on our time and place and on the future of our nation and the world.

The past decade has put the principles on which our country was founded to the test. It has given us an opportunity to look into the very workings of our democracy.

And more than that, the civil rights movement has given us an opportunity to look into our own hearts. For as John F. Kennedy said, "We are confronted with a *moral* issue. It is as old as the Scriptures and as clear as the American Constitution. The heart of the question is whether all Americans are going to be afforded equal rights and equal opportunities. *It is whether we are going to treat our fellow Americans as we want to be treated.*"

The choice is still before us.

Bibliography

Bontemps, Arna, *100 Years of Negro Freedom,* Illustrated with photographs, Dodd Mead & Co., 1961

Bontemps, Arna, *Story of the Negro,* Illustrated by Raymond Lufkin, Alfred A. Knopf, Inc., 1958

Buckmaster, Henrietta, *Freedom Bound,* The Macmillan Co., 1965

Hughes, Langston, *The First Book of Negroes,* Illustrated by Ursula Koerning, Franklin Watts, Inc., 1952

King, Martin Luther, Jr., *Why We Can't Wait,* Harper & Row Publishers, 1964

King, Martin Luther, Jr., *Stride Toward Freedom,* Harper & Row Publishers, 1958

Lomax, Louis, *The Negro Revolt,* Harper & Row Publishers, 1962 (Also paperback, Signet, New American Library)

Lubell, Samuel, *White and Black, Test of A Nation,* Harper & Row Publishers, 1964

Miers, Earl Schenck, *Freedom,* Grosset and Dunlap, Inc., 1965

Sterling, Dorothy, *Forever Free: The Story of the Emancipation Proclamation,* Illustrated by Ernest Crichlow, Doubleday & Co., Inc., 1963

Sutherland, Elizabeth, *Letters From Mississippi,* McGraw-Hill Book Co., 1965

Zinn, Howard, *SNCC The New Abolitionists,* Beacon Press, 1964

Index

Abernathy, Ralph, 39, 42, 44
Abolitionists, 7, 8, 109
Adams, John Quincy, 5, 7
Adult Education Program, 134
Aiken, George, 101
Alabama, 47, 59, 67, 81, 114
Allen, Jo Ann, 46
American Colonization Society, 17
Anthony, Susan B., 9
Arizona, 21, 47
Arkansas, 51–58
Atlanta, Ga., 58–59, 75–76, 80, 81
Attucks, Crispus, 109

"Back to Africa" movements, 16, 17
Bacon, Kay, 55–58
Baltimore, Md., 47, 70
Barnett, Ross, 61, 62, 86
Belton, Barbara, 23
Belton, Harry, 23
Bevel, James, 112, 114
Birmingham, Ala., 81, 82, 89–95
Black Codes, 10
Black Muslims, 19, 125–127
Black Nationalism, 17, 18, 125
Blaine, James G., 104
Blair, Ezell, 69, 73
Boston, Mass., 78
Boynton, Bruce, 79, 84
Boys of '76, 13
Browder, Aurelia, 44
Brown, Edmund (Pat), 132
Brown, Henry, 25
Brown, John, 7
Brown, Linda, 21, 22, 33, 121
Brown, Minnijean, 55
Brown, Oliver, 21–24, 28, 30, 122, 144

Calhoun, John C., 17
California, 78, 128–132
Chaney, James, 110–111, 115
Charlotte, N.C., 80
Chicago, Ill., 73, 119
Civil Rights Act, of 1964, 67, 96–97, 141
  of 1960, 140, 141
  of 1957, 140
Civil War, 4, 6, 9, 10
Clay, Henry, 17
Clinton, Tenn., 46–49
Colvin, Claudette, 34
College Work Study Program, 134
Connor, "Bull," 81–82, 90
Constitution, of the United States, 5, 140, 146
CORE, 70, 72–73, 78, 80, 117, 124, 128, 143
Cowling, Eli, 81
Cuffee, Paul, 17

Davis, Dorothy E., 23
Davis, Jefferson, 31
Declaration of Independence, 2
Detroit, Mich., 119, 125
Doar, John, 95
Douglass, Frederick, 8, 109
DuBois, W. E. B., 72
Dunn, O. J., 104

Eckford, Elizabeth, 52, 54
Eisenhower, Dwight D., 47, 54, 64, 82, 97
Emancipation Proclamation, 9, 137, 138
Evers, Medgar, 94, 95

Fard, W. D., 125
Farmer, James, 80, 81, 97
Faubus, Orville, 51–52, 54
Fifteenth Amendment, 11, 71, 103, 137, 139

Forman, James, 74, 108
Fourteenth Amendment, 10–11, 24, 26, 29, 71, 139
Fox, Joseph, 55
Franklin, Benjamin, 7
Free African Society, 16
Freedom Democratic Party, 114
Friedman, Seymour, 91

Gadsden, Ala., 85, 86
Gaines, Lloyd, 27
Gantt, Harvey, 64, 65, 66
Garrison, William Lloyd, 8, 13
Garvey, Marcus, 17, 24, 125
Georgia, 47, 106, 115
Ghandi, Mahatma, 40
Glascock, Thomas, 6
Goodman, Andrew, 110–111, 115
Grant, Leo, 48
Green, Ernest, 55–58
Greensboro, N. C., 68–71, 74

Hamer, Fannie Lou, 112, 113
Harlan, John Marshall, 26, 27
Harpers Ferry, Va., 7
Hollings, Ernest F., 65
Holt, Len, 70–71
HOPE, 59
Howe, Harold, 123
Hoxie, Ark., 50
Hughes, Charles Evans, 27
Humphrey, Hubert, 100

Jackson, Miss., 83–84, 94
Jamestown, Va., 4
Jenkins, Herbert, 59
Job Corps, 133
Johnson, Andrew, 9–10
Johnson, Paul B., 114
Johnson, Lyndon Baines, 1, 15, 51, 100–102, 124, 132, 135–137

Kansas, 21, 47
Kasper, John, 47–49
Katzenbach, Nicholas, 62

Kennedy, John F., 62, 63, 82, 86, 88, 95–96, 98–100, 141, 145, 146
Kennedy, Robert F., 63, 81, 82, 84
Killen, John, 19
King, A. D., 93
King, Coretta (Scott), 36, 38
King, Martin Luther, 35–45, 89–94, 98–99, 101, 129, 143–145
Knights of the White Camelia, 12
Ku Klux Klan, 12, 92, 94, 112

Lewis, John, 74, 80–81, 97
Liberia, 17
Lincoln, Abraham, 9, 99, 137
Little Rock, Ark., 51–58, 64
Los Angeles, Cal., 78, 128–132
Louisiana, 47, 104
Lovejoy, Elijah, 8

MacNeill, Joseph, 68–69, 73
Malcolm X, 126
"March on Washington," 97–99
Marshall, Burke, 92
Marshall, Thurgood, 142
McCone Commission, 132–133
Meredith, James, 60–63, 66
Mississippi, 47, 103, 106–116
Missouri, 27
Montgomery, Ala., 30–45, 71, 82–83
Moore, Amzie, 107
Moore, William, 86–88, 90, 95
Morris, R. J., 131
Moses, Bob, 107–108
Mott, Lucretia, 9
Muhammed, Elijah, 125–126

NAACP, 24, 35, 54, 61, 70–73, 76, 143
Nation of Islam (Black Muslims), 18–19, 125
Neighborhood Youth Corps, 134

New Jersey, 77
New Mexico, 21
New Rochelle, N.Y., 122
New York, N.Y., 73, 117–119,
123, 124, 127–128
Nineteenth Amendment, 8
Nixon, E. D., 35, 44

Oklahoma, 70, 105
Operation Headstart, 134
Organization of Afro-American
Unity, 126
Oxford, Miss., 60–63

Parker, Sammy Dean, 55–57
Parker, William, 130
Parks, Rosa, 33–35, 44, 97
Patterson, John, 82
Philadelphia, Pa., 124, 128
Pinckney Resolution, 7
Plessy, Homer, 24–27, 28

Quakers, 7

Raleigh, N.C., 73
Randolph, A. Philip, 20, 97
Reconstruction, 11, 13, 103–105
Revolutionary War, 5, 31
Reeb, James, 2
Richmond, Va., 79
Ricketts, Mrs. Jurunn, 55–57
Roberts, Terrence, 53
Rock Hill, S. C., 80
Roosevelt, Franklin D., 20
Rush, Benjamin, 7
Rustin, Bayard, 97

St. Louis, Mo., 70
Schwerner, Michael, 110–111,
115
SCLC, 71, 73, 143
Seattle, Wash., 78
Selma, Ala., 1–2
Shuttlesworth, Fred J., 92
Simpkins, George, 70
Smiley, Glenn, 44
SNCC, 73–74, 80, 143

South Carolina, 60, 64–66
Speed, Joshua, 9
Stanley, Thomas B., 47, 51
Stone, Lucy, 9
Stowe, Harriet Beecher, 8
Supreme Court, 3, 20, 23–32,
35, 44, 49, 79, 140
Sweatt v. Painter, 27, 28

Tennessee, 46–49, 51
Texas, 27–28, 67
Thirteenth Amendment, 4, 25,
139
Thompson, Allen C., 94
Tourgee, Albion W., 104
Truman, Harry S., 19
Truth, Sojourner, 9
Tubman, Harriet, 9, 109
Turner, Nat, 6

Underground Railroad, 109
Universal Negro Improvement
Association, 18

Vardaman, J. K., 25
Vesey, Denmark, 6
Virginia, 47, 51
Voting Rights Act of 1965, 116,
137

Walker, Wyatt T., 93
Warren, Earl, 29–30, 144
Washington, D.C., 32, 47, 77,
97–99
Washington, George, 138
Watts (Los Angeles), Cal., 128–
132
Weaver, Robert C., 135, 142
White Citizens Councils, 50, 51
Whitney, Eli, 6
Wilkins, Roger W., 135
Wilkins, Roy, 96, 135
Wilson, Woodrow, 27
Woods, Robin, 55–57
Woodward, C. Zann, 142
Woolman, John, 7

Young, Whitney, 97